PRAISE FOR

Better

Caldwell reminds us of the oft-ignored power of spirituality and art in making personal and planetary change — and gives readers a practical philosophy of how to do so, via a touching memoir of how she figured it out herself. You'll walk away from *Better* inspired and enlightened.

—Starre Vartan, founder and editor, *Eco-Chick*

We need to explore new models of living with greater respect for the earth and our fellow earthlings, both human and nonhuman. *Better* describes how to live more consciously and harmoniously. It engages our hearts and aspirations, while also providing practical advice for developing healthy habits. Fundamentally, the book urges us to live mindfully and according to the best of our humanity, and ultimately to make the world a better place.

—Gene Baur, President and Co-Founder, Farm Sanctuary

Wow, am I excited about this book! I expected the usual depressing list of problems and boring list of solutions, but was I wrong. I was surprised and delighted! Nicole Caldwell is a great writer, creative thinker and — in particular — a good storyteller. I came away feeling expanded and hopeful — inspired by her ability to communicate exuberance for new ideas and by her belief in our ability to change — especially her faith in the idea that we are "better together."

—Cecile Andrews, author, *Living Room Revolution*, *Less Is More*, *Slow Is Beautiful*, and *Circle of Simplicity*

NO LONGER PROPERTY OF
SEATTLE PUBLIC LIBRARY

Provocative, practical and inspiring, Nicole Caldwell's *Better* will put a spring in your step as you head into your garden or community to become the artist of life we're all destined to be. In so doing, we can transform the world for the better.

—John D. Ivanko and Lisa Kivirist, co-authors,
Homemade for Sale and *Farmstead Chef*

Feeling stressed and trapped in a no-win world? Curl up with a cup of tea and this book and begin dreaming of a sustainable future in a better world.

—Deborah Niemann, author,
Homegrown and Handmade and *Ecothrifty*

Better

Better

the everyday art
of sustainable living

Nicole Caldwell

new society
PUBLISHERS

**Copyright © 2015 by Nicole Caldwell.
All rights reserved.**

Cover design by Diane McIntosh.
Wooden Frame © iStock robynmac. Beach background © iStock titlezpix

Printed in Canada. First printing May 2015.

New Society Publishers acknowledges the financial support of the Government of Canada through the Canada Book Fund (CBF) for our publishing activities.

Paperback ISBN: 978-0-86571-794-7
eISBN: 978-1-55092-587-6

Inquiries regarding requests to reprint all or part of *Better* should be addressed to New Society Publishers at the address below. To order directly from the publishers, please call toll-free (North America) 1-800-567-6772, or order online at www.newsociety.com

Any other inquiries can be directed by mail to:
New Society Publishers
P.O. Box 189, Gabriola Island, BC V0R 1X0, Canada
(250) 247-9737

New Society Publishers' mission is to publish books that contribute in fundamental ways to building an ecologically sustainable and just society, and to do so with the least possible impact on the environment, in a manner that models this vision. We are committed to doing this not just through education, but through action. The interior pages of our bound books are printed on Forest Stewardship Council®-registered acid-free paper that is **100% post-consumer recycled** (100% old growth forest-free), processed chlorine-free, and printed with vegetable-based, low-VOC inks, with covers produced using FSC®-registered stock. New Society also works to reduce its carbon footprint, and purchases carbon offsets based on an annual audit to ensure a carbon neutral footprint. For further information, or to browse our full list of books and purchase securely, visit our website at: www.newsociety.com

Library and Archives Canada Cataloguing in Publication

Caldwell, Nicole, author
        Better : the everyday art of sustainable living / Nicole Caldwell.

Includes bibliographical references and index.
Issued in print and electronic formats.
ISBN 978-0-86571-794-7 (paperback).--ISBN 978-1-55092-587-6 (ebook)

        1. Sustainable living. I. Title.

GE196.C34 2015   640   C2015-902828-0
                                                         C2015-902829-9

Contents

Introduction

*Only after the last tree has been cut down, only after the
last river has been poisoned, only after the last fish
has been caught — only then will you find
that your money cannot be eaten.*

— Cree Indian Prophecy

A Single Step

B *ETTER* IS A BOOK ABOUT HOPE.
This is a book about reconnecting to our animalness. Our humanness.
There is no shortage of books outlining bleak environmental theory.
Better on the other hand was written to inspire you to create change
in your everyday life that will in turn inspire people around you to
make changes. *Better* depends on the power of each of us to have more
purpose, be more joyful, more empathic and more loving to the Earth
and each other. We need to understand where we went wrong, and we
need the imagination to do better. *Better* provides a bird's-eye view of
the desperate state the natural world's in and offers pragmatic options
for changing that status quo one sustainable, creative action at a time.

Better invites you to change your perceptions and see adversity as
opportunity. Instead of thinking outside the box, this book wants you
to destroy the box entirely and ditch it in your compost pile. *Hasta
la vista. See ya later, Alligator. C'est la vie. Better* is about reimagining

what our lives can be and repairing our relationship with the environment. This book is a call to arms: to take chances, bark at the moon, use less, play more, grow food, heed the power of coincidence, smile at strangers and turn your life into your greatest artistic achievement. Because no amount of doom and gloom can change the fact that a land of opportunity awaits us. When we change our perceptions and how we frame them, we change the world. It's like the fortune cookie says: "Everything you are against weakens you. Everything you are for empowers you."

All change begins with the acknowledgment of facts. We must fess up. It is time for us to admit what we are doing to each other, the planet and ourselves. Anxiety is bred from the outer edges of awareness — a refusal to look at and address hard issues at hand. It is time for us to empower ourselves to stare our situation right in the face, understand the problems and make new plans. This is a painful process. It is not easy to own up. It's not easy to open Pandora's box. And sometimes, solutions are hard to come by.

But everything starts in the dark. Changing our lives means reconnecting to ethics that exist above the plane of cultural *normalcy*. We have to stop acting as though over-consumption is *The American Way* — somehow a natural or god-given right. Our true rights and responsibilities lie in our ability to be enlightened, vulnerable, compassionate beings living in cooperation with the people and world around us. This is a cure to our isolation and a real road to fulfillment and purpose.

To anchor these perspectives, *Better* makes it personal with stories of people just like you and me who found ways to transition into more creative, sustainable ways of life. People who opted out of stagnancy. People who flipped the bird to hardships and demanded happiness over complacency. I'll also share the story of the farm where I live, and my own move from city to country. Transforming my uncle's commune into a sustainability campus and artist colony has been a crash course in the lessons of the Better Theory, a philosophy you are about to know a whole lot about.

All routes are not the same and I'm not encouraging you all to quit your jobs, ditch your relationships and head to the country to start churning out a field of veggies and offering your home up to a bunch of artists. But I am encouraging you to look at your life differently. I'm inviting you to change your relationship to the planet.

Throughout *Better*, I refer to the problems *we* face and the environmental issues *we* have created. I realize we are not all the same: not all living without concern for the world around us, not all in utter isolation from our neighbors and families. Many of the issues discussed in *Better* apply to relatively wealthier demographics who may have televisions in every room, big lawns, multiple family vehicles and other amenities most people in this world will never have — and may not want. The use of *we* throughout *Better* is a tool designed to make cultural issues universal. Environmental problems don't exist in a vacuum, any more than behavioral problems or personality disorders do. We are all affected by each other and the world we live in. So *we* refers to our culture in general — the global culture — and invites each of us to bear the responsibility of all of us, across all living situations, demographics and personalities. *We* as a global community have pushed ourselves to the edge. *We* as humans have out-consumed our natural resources. *We* together should be seeking out creative solutions. Those solutions can often be enacted by a whole lot of people no matter their lifestyles, income levels or geography. We can all think about the ingredients in our toiletries, cleaning products and fertilizers. We can all think of ways to give back more to Mother Earth.

Art holds many meanings for different people. In the title of this book, *art* refers to any action done well. There is an art to everything — so why not to our own lives? Living intentionally, growing out of the Earth and sharing happiness with the people around us are art forms. Sustainable living deals specifically with the total celebration of life — one centered around growth, love and compassion for all living things, including ourselves.

I've heard lots of people say the human race is past the point of no return; that we may as well throw in the towel. But if we can't change everything, is it really appropriate to change nothing? The deepest satisfaction does not always lie in what you get out of x, y or z as a result of your work. The working is the reward. The journey is the gift. A small change is still a change. We transform the world each time we give. Each time we choose love. Each time we grow, cultivate and build. Doomsday attitudes make us lazy. A life of complacency is no life at all.

You don't love in a real way for what you will get in return. You love not because a person will inherently love you back or because you have some selfish need for them; instead you might know how to love them well in a way they wouldn't otherwise experience. You do these things for them, but you can't help ending up a little wiser, a littler kinder and a little better off yourself for loving another. The act of love itself is transformative. It's not a cash deal or barter. You love someone completely and utterly for free. Sometimes you get burned. And if you're smart, when you're all done crying into a pillow and licking your wounds, you go out and you love some more.

Maybe you play sports. Maybe you're not a star. But maybe a person you play with or against is going to one day turn pro. And maybe during practice, you're actually in some way helping to thrust that player on to bigger things. Maybe that's your contribution: not to have been the best yourself, but to have been the one who pushed the others who go on to become giants.

There is a parable about an old man who walked along a beach the morning after a storm. Starfish were stranded along the sand as the tide went out. In the distance, the man saw a little girl throwing starfish one at a time out into the waves. He walked up to her. "Why are you throwing starfish into the ocean?" he asked. "The sun is up and the tide is low," she replied. "If I don't throw them back into the water, the starfish will die." The man shook his head. "Do you not realize there are miles of beach and thousands of starfish? You cannot possibly make a difference." The girl smiled, picked up another starfish and threw it into the sea. She looked the old man straight in the eye. "It made a difference to that one."

This book is about small steps. It's about turning darkness into silver linings and making positive changes wherever possible, with the faith that those small pieces make huge differences. It's about creating art for art's sake, loving for love's sake, and it's about worshiping the dirt, the air and the water. It's about finding whimsy, coincidence and magic in your everyday life. It's about paying attention to moments and seeing them as opportunities and gifts. It's about picking up one starfish at a time and tossing it back out to sea.

The greatest losses — and gains — in the world come in a flood of tiny instances. The recipe for life's complexities is comprised of the smallest, and at times seemingly insignificant, details. And as *Better* may show you, some of humanity's greatest turning points have occurred in the face of adversity and tragedy. Our moments of extreme opportunity often stem from the darkest times.

You do no service to the world by diminishing yourself. Character is always destiny. Each of us is capable of turning a negative into a positive. It isn't too late. In fact, it's the perfect time. It's here. It's now. It's Better.

We have arrived at a moment of reckoning. The question is, what will we do with it?

Our Disconnect

We're plugged in. We're turned on. And we're completely disconnected.

We spend more time scrolling through social media sites or checking our phones than we spend with our friends. We're inside more than we're outside. We keep our muscles toned in gyms, not by active lifestyles. The television is filled with talking heads arguing over politics, reality TV, gun laws and the ever-loosening fabric of our society and culture. We worry more about money than the environment.

Many of us have forgotten who we are on a literal level. We pad our brains with patriotism, pop culture and painkillers in a subconscious gesture to ignore The American Dream's disappointing, diminishing return. We're pissed off, we're isolated, we're fat and we're lonelier than we've ever been. We have gone so far in the wrong direction that we've somehow programmed our brains to defend our present way of life in the US even as it kills us.

We worry about our waistlines but not where our food came from. We debate politics but not clean water. We divide ourselves by political party, race, musical tastes, ages and income levels. We lose sleep over new smart phone and video game releases, not over air quality. We practice idolatry of celebrities while neglecting the very ground beneath our feet. We are more concerned about buying than about what we leave behind.

Everything in the universe is made out of the same five basic elements: air, fire, water, earth and ether. All living things have utilized other living organisms and molecules to survive over and over again. What we do to the planet, we do to ourselves. Everything is connected.

Religion was born from the natural world. Stars in the night sky, volcanic eruption, illness, miracles, dimples and rainbows: all came from the earth and sky, and all were believed to be signs of a higher power, a godliness. So much of religion involves food: a recognition of the sacrifice one living thing makes to the next — plant to animal to human, or a variation therein. One thing gives its life so the next may eat. At the end of that chain, there is death and decomposition and the cycle repeats. We have no problem proselytizing and belonging to a sect; yet we forget why that sect exists in the first place, forget that all religions are based in the natural world. We worship the branches of our planet — gods, spirituality and religion in general — without worshiping the roots.

We've forgotten the natural order of things. To civilize the terrain, men carved trails of tears then paved paradise for a flurry of golden highways, strip malls and fast food outlets. We pay no heed to the weather, the seasons, the length of days or moon cycles, save for how these issues affect our wardrobes or social lives. Most of us don't know whether it's a good year for tomatoes, if there's a blight on elm trees or if there are algal blooms in our local lakes. We don't know how the honeybees or bats are doing. We don't know how the soil is in our own backyards.

This isn't right. It isn't normal. And it's not how we ever used to do things.

For most of human existence, *garbage* was comprised of biodegradable items like clay pots or animal hides. When a person died, he or she wasn't pumped with preservatives and then buried as some strange, toxic seed in the ground. Items were manufactured to last. Once we learned some basic agriculture, people grew their own food as a matter of course. Victory gardens in people's backyards during World II accounted for a full 40% of vegetables produced in the US in 1944.[1]

Until very recently, many people in the US knew by the age of 18 how to safely handle a firearm, milk a cow, repair a piece of clothing, split firewood, make basic repairs, cultivate a garden, hammer a nail and prepare food.[2] In the grand scheme of human evolution, we've only been living as unskilled as we do now, as distinctly set apart from nature, for a couple of centuries. That's a blip on the radar. A grain of sand on the beach of time.

In order to do any human things — to make civilizations and destroy them, obsess over material gains, build great skyscrapers and jet set and work a nine-to-five job, lobby congress, invest and gamble and win and lose — we have to, fundamentally, be able to breathe and eat and have shelter. Before we can worry about job loss in the US or our footing in the international economy, we would be wise to remember we're animals who need certain things in order to survive. We have to inhale and exhale, drink water and swallow food. And the more we poison that which provides those things, the closer we bring ourselves to the point of no more life. That's literal.

We button ourselves away in homes, each of which must have its own washing machine, dishwasher, lawnmower, several air conditioners and televisions, a furnace, hot water heater and swimming pool. We consume instead of produce. We have lost ourselves entirely to a world emphasizing money and consumption over mindfulness and compassion. What's the endgame? A satirical zoo exhibit of humans in their constructed habitats looking more like a movie set than a world, without any speakable future. The emperor has no clothes. The cat's out of the bag. The vandals took the handles.

In the short-term we can rely on water treatment plants; they allow the richest people to drink the best water money can buy while actual water bodies are polluted. We can continue chemically treating lawns so they're zapped of organic matter but look green and healthy. We can frack for natural gas and continue to pull oil out of the ground. We can use treated, drinkable water to flush human waste to a septic or processing plant. We can make more and more car factories, farm salmon indoors and we can break apart mountains to mine pretty bands of gold that prove how in love we are. We can upgrade our smart phones every two years and buy new laptops every three. We can stay comfortable with the planned obsolescence of all the crap we buy, throw away and buy again.

We can continue getting meat from companies that operate factory farms and shoot said product up with pink slime to keep prices down and food in high supply. We can purchase vegetables from halfway around the world and eat apples that have been sprayed with god-knows-what so they are without a single blemish. We can keep doing these things, but while our heads are in the sand the One Great Truth is that these things, done in these ways, simply can't go on forever. The system itself is unsustainable. Too much is being taken, and too many toxins are being given back. It's a one-way, dead-end street.

Sustainability refers to an action that can be repeated indefinitely, constantly replenishing what is being taken. If we do things that don't complement that design, eventually the system fails. The longer we choose industry over environment, jobs over air, corporate loopholes over water, well, the less sustainable we are. We can't keep pushing the pesky issue of finite natural resources out of the way to maintain some standard of living that is just wholly out of step with our animalness. Doing so secures only one thing: that we're going to run out of the very things we need the most even sooner.

A culture based on so-called infinite growth is doomed. The game is rigged. And yet we stay inside this ill-formed framework and think we can bring about real change. We can't. The current state of Big Agriculture, our relationships with the land around us, our politics and our separation from the very communities we live in have got to change completely if we actually want to leave things richer than we found them.

It's overwhelming, isn't it? Seems safe to say we're a hopeless case. Glaciers are already melting, we're watching more extreme weather roll through each year, and the population is going in only one direction. Will it be our overuse of cars or rainforests cleared for cattle that will be our undoing? Will it be fracking? An oil pipeline? We're coming too close for comfort to a cliff edge we're just beginning to clearly see.

But what if I told you we have a choice? We are not kittens up a tree or damsels in distress. We actually have a hand in this game. We can live comfortably, happily and safely without diminishing the natural world. We can stop being part of the problem. We can change the rules and save ourselves. We can still make things Better.

All we have to do is start.

Part 1

Ah, the world! Oh, the world!

— Herman Melville

Mundus vult decipi.
The world wants to be deceived.

— Latin proverb

Hardships often prepare ordinary people
for an extraordinary destiny.

— C.S. Lewis

The earth's atrot! The sun's a scream!
The air's a jig. The water's great!

— James Joyce

They tried to bury us.
They didn't know we were seeds.

— Mexican proverb

Chapter 1

The Better Theory

I N THE BETTER THEORY, every experience is a teacher. Crisis teaches you cool, pain teaches you pleasure, loss teaches you love. Every large and small and good and bad happening offers countless opportunities to grow, expand, let go and learn: in a nutshell, to be better.

Each trauma, eerie coincidence, tragedy, missed bus, layoff, breakup or failure has something to show you. The answers to all our questions lie in the events of our everyday lives; the Better Theory teaches us the significance of each occurrence.

People's perceptions transform experiences. How one looks at the world alters that world wholly. If you look at the next bad thing that happens in your life as an opportunity to grow and learn, you will grow and learn from it. If you keep this concept with you, you'll find countless chances every day to improve your life and your surroundings. You will also see how others throughout history and storybooks have used the Better Theory to achieve the seemingly impossible: that Joan of Arc would of course employ her visions to lead the French military; that Frodo Baggins would utilize his perspectives as a simple hobbit to save the world and that David had the edge on Goliath the whole time.

We generally consider hardships to be disadvantages — experiences to be loathed and avoided at all costs. With this conventional wisdom, anything that is difficult or painful works against us. Yet history tells a much different story.

Twelve of the first 44 US presidents at a young age lost their fathers. Albert Einstein didn't start speaking until he was four years old. Benjamin Franklin dropped out of school when he was ten because his parents could no longer afford his education. Ella Fitzgerald — along with other celebrities like Halle Berry, Jewel, Dr. Phil, Jim Carrey, Harry Houdini and Charlie Chaplin — experienced homelessness. Stephen King's first novel, *Carrie,* was rejected 30 times. Oprah Winfrey was sexually abused as a child, became pregnant at 14 and lost the baby in its infancy.

An astounding number of successful business people struggled early in life to overcome dyslexia. Just a few include Cisco CEO John Chambers, cell phone pioneer Craig McCaw, JetBlue founder David Neelemna, Kinkos founder Paul Orfalea and discount brokerage firm founder Charles Schwab. In his book *David and Goliath: Underdogs, Misfits, and the Art of Battling Giants,* Malcolm Gladwell suggested that instead of succeeding in spite of their learning disabilities, these moguls triumphed precisely because of them. Their battles with their disorders taught them some things that became assets.

Of course no one wants to point to trauma or extreme hardship as a requisite for success. And of course those of us who grew up in loving, nurturing homes with creature comforts enjoyed the advantages of protection, security and support. All those benefits can certainly help a person become successful and happy in the world. But choosing to muscle through the most difficult human experiences bolsters directness, toughness, pride and the ability to creatively solve problems. And those too, Gladwell argues, are necessary ingredients for success.

Where would we be without the blues, anyway? Without struggle, hardship or broken hearts there would be no music. No art. Without the blues there would be no Billie Holiday. No Ray Charles. No Hank Williams, Elvis Presley or Etta James. Without the blues we'd be without Van Gogh, Frida Kahlo and Picasso. Bad stuff that happens is the grit in our bellies we can choose to use as fuel for our creative process.

It's tempting to turn negatives into energy vacuums. Something bad happens, and we use it as a chance to pull attention from people around us. We complain. We act out. We manipulate. In the short term, this can feel like we're getting *a fix.* But in reality, we're damaging everyone involved. There is another way to meet our needs. Instead of staying broken and seeking instant gratification, we can choose to heal. Instead of wearing our tribulations as armor, they can become tools to aid us in expanding ourselves so we don't need armor. We can forgive ourselves our weaknesses and begin the often-challenging process of moving on.

Rory McIlroy, a young pro golfer from Northern Ireland, was winning the 2011 Masters Golf Tournament in Augusta, Georgia. Most professional players go their whole lives without winning any round in the majors, but McIlroy at just 21 years old and without any prior victories was enjoying a safe lead on the final day. But on the back nine, McIlroy choked. He shot a triple-bogey on No. 10 and proceeded to shoot the worst day of golf in his four-year career. He tied for 15th place and was all but laughed off the course. It was painful to watch.

Because McIlroy came so close and lost so dramatically, most people thought he'd never win a major. Many thought McIlroy would become a head case in a sport played largely in the six inches between one's ears. After the loss at Augusta, the young golfer was forced to interview for the public media. Reflecting on his worst day in his professional career, McIlroy chose to quote Muhammed Ali: "It's repetition of affirmations that leads to belief — and once that belief becomes a deep conviction, things begin to happen." Three months later, McIlroy won the US Open. But he did more than win: he shattered almost every record associated with that tournament.

For as long as we have kept history alive through storytelling and writing, so too have we used mythology to tell tales of individuals who triumph over tragedy or seeming disadvantages to become successful. Movies and literature document countless tales of overcoming obstacles and underdogs having their day at the top.

Ill-equipped rebels take on — and beat — the Empire in *Star Wars.* Peter Parker faces down the side effect of an insect bite by becoming Spider-Man. In Roald Dahl's story and the film made from it, Matilda overcomes adversity by reading and teaching herself telekinesis — a talent that allows her to come out on top. The tortoise beats the hare. In *Even Cowgirls Get the Blues,* Sissy Hankshaw takes a deformity — grotesquely oversized thumbs — and turns it into an advantage.

In *Star Trek II: The Wrath of Khan,* a Starfleet Academy training exercise called the Kobayashi Maru tests the gumption and poise of cadets when faced with a no-win scenario. In this flight-simulation exercise, a cadet in command of the USS *Enterprise* receives a distress signal stating that civilian freighter *Kobayashi Maru* has hit a gravitic mine in the Klingon Neutral Zone and is losing power and life support. Cadets must choose to attempt a rescue of the *Kobayashi Maru* or abandon it, as the test by design offers no way to rescue the freighter and get out of the neutral zone without inciting a fatal battle with Klingon ships.

The test itself is interesting, but what makes the *Kobayashi Maru* simulation in this story great is how cadet James T. Kirk beats it. Before he undertakes the exercise for a third time (after failing twice), Kirk manages to reprogram the simulator so it's actually possible to rescue the *Kobayashi Maru.* Kirk is awarded a commendation for original thinking. He effectively changed the rules of the game in order to create a different outcome rather than play within the confines of an unworkable system.

That's the purpose of the Better Theory: to redefine what we would normally consider a negative or no-win scenario and turn it into an opportunity for greatness. And that's the goal of the work I do at Better Farm: to take all the environmental obstacles and cultural isolation we're faced with in this world and use them as lessons in how to transcend them.

This isn't to say we should wish for bad things — or that when bad things happen we should somehow act like they're no big deal. The same trauma that invigorates one person may overpower another. But what we gain by going through tough times and coming out on the other side is courage. When we're in agony, we become willing to take chances we don't when we're comfortable. We suddenly discover a feeling of urgency and thrilling sense of freedom. We get to make new rules. And the people who come out on the other side are the same people who emerge as leaders in their fields, innovative thinkers and joyful individuals.

The world needs people like this.

All you've got to do is climb aboard, hang on tight and push your-self forward into the abyss. It's a tricky theory to test-drive; rarely do you say "Better" first thing after something terrible happens. But the truth is, Better works.

French pharmacist and psychologist Émile Coué trailblazed the idea of *conscious autosuggestion* when in 1910 he began a series of ex-periments in which he had subjects repeat the mantra "Every day, in every way, I am getting better and better" (in French: Tous les jours, à tous points de vue, je vais de mieux en mieux).

John Lennon fans among you may recognize Coué's mantra from the 1980 song "Beautiful Boy."

The people in Coué's experiment were to recite the line 20 times each morning before getting out of bed and again each night before falling asleep. Subjects' eyes had to be closed, and the line was to be spoken in a whispered monotone.

Coué's goal? To improve rehabilitation for people who had experi-enced physical or emotional distress. Roots of the Coué method came from his discovery that his patients' bodies responded better to medica-tions when Coué made a point to praise their effectiveness. Theorizing that patients internalized the optimistic suggestion, he began to explore the powers of the imagination to facilitate physical and mental healing.

Coué felt the key to wellness lies in an individual's ability to change his or her unconscious thoughts through imagination. Sound familiar?

C. Harry Brooks, who wrote a number of books about Coué and his work, estimated the success rate of this practice at 93%. Those suc-cesses included people suffering from atrophy, organ problems, trauma, diabetes and many other physical ailments. Coué's subjects were, ulti-mately, able to heal themselves.

Jimmy Nicol was a stand-in drummer for the Beatles during their 1964 tour of Europe, Hong Kong and Australia while Ringo was in a hospital nursing tonsillitis. Nicol was known for using the phrase "It's getting better," which would go on to inspire Paul McCartney's lyrics for the group's hit "Getting Better." Lennon and McCartney wrote the verses for that chorus; and as McCartney sang the refrain "Getting better all the time;" Lennon threw in the line "It can't get any worse."

While the title points to the optimistic (better), the verses refer to an "angry young man," schoolroom disobedience and violence.

Because it is the negative that informs the positive. This is the tension of Better.

Losses will often give more than gains. Losses wake us up. In a miserable marriage? Have a job you loathe? Personal life uninspiring? Pay attention to what you feel uneasy about. That voice is your inner self telling your outer self to get this show on the road. The Better Theory is about realizing that your life is bigger than any one of these negatives. These negatives are going to push you where you are meant to go. We have lots of words for this like fate, ambition and finding one's path. It's all Better.

The Engaged Buddhism movement, founded by Zen Buddhist teacher Thich Nhat Hanh, invites individuals to draw from their teachings to facilitate change on social, political and environmental platforms. The movement pushes practitioners beyond meditation in order to encourage outside action: boycotts, protests and grassroots activity. The practice allows people to address their personal fears and limitations before taking on exterior adversity.

For the Engaged Better movement, your challenge is similar: to ditch the complexities and utter busy-ness of today's consumer-based society and sign on the dotted line for fun. For mischief. For joy. The Better Theory is about grabbing the reins. It's about using your struggles to inform your successes. It's about no longer waiting for humankind to improve, instead living like that day is here. You be the outlaw. Let humanity catch up to you.

The Better Theory is your ticket out of all the things that bind you. It's a reminder you can turn even your worst misery or mistake into your most enlightened teacher. Heed the Better Theory, and those things entering your life of which you are most afraid become your partners in crime in a car chase toward Enlightenment. You'll be choreographing dance moves for your demons in no time — and counteracting this planet's bad case of the blues with a little bit of green.

Chapter 2

Lending Yourself to Infinity

A SUSTAINABLE ACT is one you can repeat forever in the same way. That's it. For all the attention sustainability gets nowadays, the concept itself is so simple, it's amazing the practice eludes even our most educated politicians and world leaders.

Sustainability is literally the act of lending oneself to infinity.

Sustainability is the capacity to endure. Something is put into the system, something is taken out of the system, and this give-and-take creates a perfectly symbiotic occurrence that can be done and done again. A plant grows in the dirt and from the sun, it releases beneficial nutrients back into the earth, it filters the air, it gains life from what's around it and it gives life back. This is how forests are formed — and how they last, save for an ice age or the flick of a chainsaw.

Sustainability refers to more than the environment. It refers to all who are part of the environment, including us. Our highest ideals are all bred out of sustainability. Look at just about every holy book from all time. Religions promote sustainability on a spiritual level: that we would be responsible stewards of the Earth, treat each other as we'd like to be treated, not commit trespasses, offer forgiveness, be gentle and love each other. Yet we are overwhelmed by the choices we face in our daily lives. We turn against one another. Our minds are totally cluttered with anxieties and fears. We are using the Earth's resources almost one and a half times as quickly as nature can replenish them. This is not sustainable.

Somewhere along the way, the connection between science and spirituality became fractured. The precursor to chemistry and speculative philosophy was alchemy; where individuals learned the scientific process and how it connected to the transformation of the human soul. Alchemy, integral to the development of early modern science, bridged the natural world and spirituality. Concepts of alchemy are mirrored on the physical plane and the spiritual self.

It's time to reconnect planet and human, science and heart. We are all in this together. And in order to heal the world, we will have to also work on us. It is time to stop seeking happiness in a vocation, job, location or partner and instead realize that the cure lies within. It is time to discover the sacredness that exists in every mundane moment instead of thinking we'd be more fulfilled if only if we had this or that. It is time to stop seeing the environment and threats against it as outside of ourselves. We are not on the Earth; we are *of* the Earth.

How can we find Better in the haze of our busy, daily lives?

Our breath. A good stretch. The touch of skin-on-skin. A perfect breeze. The sound of rain falling. When we focus on these simple pleasures, we approach a more sustainable life of mindfulness and gentleness. If we focus on the energy we receive from our food, we think more about where the food came from and what kind of vitality that food contains. We follow chains of energy and suddenly may not want to eat certain things or be around certain people. Others, we are drawn to. This becomes our path.

Every microbe, bacteria, atom and animal on Earth has the concept of sustainability down pat. Every animal, that is, except for one. Why is it so difficult for humans to live within and because of the world instead of pushing on in spite of it?

We have turned nature into *the other* — separate from human beings, who we see as somehow exempt from natural order. This creates a break between the two ideas. Our separation from each other is a further fragmentation. And we wonder why incidents of depression, addiction and violence occur in record numbers?

From before the Industrial Revolution right up until the latter half of the 20th century, we humans have carried on as though natural resources were indispensable. Things have changed. As a global culture we have finally come to realize that ecosystems like rainforests, coral reefs and forests are exhaustible. We have seen the ecological effects of irresponsible mineral and fuel extractions. We have watched as islands of plastic form in our oceans. We have witnessed firsthand what happens when too many people try to use too much and give too little back. Yet instead of limiting our harm and reducing our desires, we ask technology to provide us with new ways to always consume more.

Solastasia is a term referring to environmentally induced distress. Philosopher Glenn Albrecht coined the word in 2003 to define the existential anguish caused by environmental change that's amplified by a sense of powerlessness.[1] Many of us suffer from solastasia without realizing it. The condition appears to be something else that we can't pinpoint. Meanwhile the world around us continues dying, and we are more stressed than ever before, more anxious and more fearful.

Think of every system you participate in on a daily basis: the water pumped through your home that you use for your sink, shower, toilet and drinking; the food you eat every day and where it came from; your modes of transportation; how you heat and cool your house and how much you throw away. Look at your relationships, how you treat the people in your life and how they treat you.

Most of our actions are unsustainable, linear instead of circular. We take from the Earth and each other more than we give. With a very large population out-consuming its resources, that track becomes a dead-end street.

What major resources do we need in order to remain alive?

- Air
- Water
- Food

And beyond that, what do we require in order to thrive?

- Love
- Community
- Connection

We mirror our relationships with the natural world in our relationships with each other. We are part of a culture that has used up and drained natural resources and then gone and done the same thing to people. We are as unconcerned with what we leave behind as with who our neighbors are.

Instead of closing the loop and giving back to the Earth in parts equal or greater to our consumption, we cheat. We artificially grow super crops and depend on large-scale, international agriculture to feed us. We live in unnecessary luxury and pay more heed to money than common sense. If we overfish an ocean, we create farms to raise fish. If a landfill overflows, we make another. When we extract all the ore or coal or gold from a mountain, we find a different one to level. We burn bridges at work and take our lovers for granted. We don't give back to any system at the same rate we take.

There's a cost for living like this. We part with the well-being of animals, crops and people in order to always take more. Meanwhile the stuff we eat, the fuels we use, the clean air we breathe, the fresh water we drink and the energy we steal are all running out. There are just too many of us using, eating, breathing and taking out of the system without putting enough back in for the relationship not to exhaust its partners. Based on the current system, there is no question we will run out of the basic resources required to support a population of our size, in the way we consume now. Life as we know it in the developed world will end. A design based on unlimited growth with limited natural resources is a design destined for failure.

We've got a serious problem here: the perfect storm of overpopulation, too much strain on natural resources, accelerated climate change and simply not enough space to maintain the status quo.

The area where my farm is located is known the world over as the Thousand Islands Region, but also has several other names. Canadians call it the Garden of the Gods, and the Iroquois who once comprised the majority population of the land call it the Garden of the Great Spirit because of its booming harvests and unrivaled beauty. Better Farm is situated among 18 natural lakes and just 10 miles from the St. Lawrence Seaway and Canadian border in Redwood, New York. The scene is a naturalist's paradise. Low population numbers have shielded locals from witnessing the same environmental degradation seen in other communities downstate and across the world. And that has meant years of irresponsible land stewardship without visible consequences.

That's changing. A heady combination of sewage treatment plants, ill-designed septic systems, overpopulation, overfishing, lax zoning, chemical dumping over the course of many decades and limited environmental education have finally begun to catch up with this Northern New York community. Back roads bear bags of household garbage dumped by people dodging fees at the local transfer station. Fish populations dwindled enough to warrant annual restocking and habitat restoration by the New York State Department of Environmental Conservation (DEC) and other organizations. The DEC now advises on how much — and what size — fish are safe to eat out of the waterways. Algal blooms, invasive species explosions and environmental hazard designations have all become par for the course in Redwood and surrounding communities that still, to the naked eye, seem largely untouched by human hands.

These issues mirror others happening on every corner of the planet right now. People have begun to take notice. We're starting to connect the dots. And the conversation has begun: How do we fix what we've altered?

In ecology, resiliency is the ability to take a punch and recover. By studying resiliency, we're able to determine what an ecosystem can bear before collapsing from too much damage. Experts figure out ecological resiliency by looking at what are referred to as *junctures* — the intersections between regenerative forces' outputs and inputs to that ecosystem from pollutants. For example, one could study an ecosystem's soil content, air quality, forest density, biomass and such and then see how those elements relate with antagonistic forces (air pollution, runoff, sewage overflows, littering). If I am the only person living in an ecosystem, chances are that ecosystem will be extremely resilient against any waste I produce.

Crowd the same ecosystem with large numbers of people, and its resiliency decreases. That's the situation we're in now. We need to come up with new solutions to deal with the natural world's every-decreasing resiliency to the hurt we're causing.

Real change starts with education and a legitimate sense of personal connection to a space. These first steps invite further action. We don't all have to be scientists or have environmental degrees to understand how critical our situation is. Our reality is troubling. But we are helpless to change things if we don't have the facts. The information we need to arm ourselves with must become common knowledge. If the media won't consistently report on environmental issues, and if schools won't teach them, then it's on us to educate each other. What emerges from this knowledge base is that a sense of community is the best cure for isolation and a new form of currency; that creativity and vulnerability are the shortest routes to opening up our hearts; and that small, biologically diverse farms are going to be our best hope for providing human food in the future.

Creativity, empathy, understanding and a team effort are just some of the attributes we need to tap into to make things better. We have to ditch the old frameworks and come up with some newer, smarter ideas. Wake up! Look outside! All of our answers are there.

It doesn't take a lot to learn the basics of what's going on in our backyards. All the crises we face dramatically improve if we become willing to make some basic changes in how we conduct ourselves at home and in our communities. Watch how a culture deals with the natural world, and you will have great insights into that culture's relationship with its own people.

Soil

Soil is the Earth's skin. It's the holy grail of ecosystems. Dirt is Ground Zero for diversity: living organisms and non-living elements Kumbaya-ing in perfect harmony.

When we discuss some of our most prominent environmental crises, soil is too often left out of the conversation. Yet soil offers water retention and filtration, climate control, acts as a growing medium (and food source) for all plant life, filters toxins, and absorbs water for uptake by plants and evaporation. It is the basis of our food security.

Soil exists in so many places and has such a vital role, in fact, that it contains the lion's share of genetic diversity on the planet.

A healthy soil depends on rot. Decay, decomposition and death are what provide the earth with the nutrients necessary for all growth and health. When plants and animals die, their bodies break down and give nutrients to the dirt, which gives nutrients to the plants and animals, and the process repeats itself. This is a sustainable system.

Earliest versions of our human relatives trotted bipedally more than three million years ago out of evolutionary soup, out of their autobiographical stint as apes and into a new role as bull in the china shop of Planet Earth.

One of the biggest victims of that manifest destiny was soil which has lost a full one third of its volume since humans became self-appointed kings of Earth's castle. It can take more than 500 years to create about one inch of topsoil; it takes far fewer to destroy it. The United Nations Food and Agriculture Organization (UNFAO) projects that the world by 2050 will have only one quarter of the topsoil it had in 1960; we could run out of the stuff 20 years after that.[2]

When we rip out all the trees in an area, plow a field, refuse to compost and practice intensive, monoculture farming, we kill topsoil. Root structures of trees help filter water from heavy rains and retain topsoil that would otherwise erode or be washed as sediment into water bodies. Floods sweep topsoil from the ground and destroy everything downstream. The scorched earth left behind is malnourished and bitter. Dried, unprotected soil gets blown away: turning literally to dust in the wind.

By not turning our food scraps into dirt, we deny soil the chance to regenerate. In the US, we lose almost three tons of topsoil per acre every single year. We produce so many corn and soybean plants to feed animals raised for meat that we cost ourselves an estimated $45 billion annually in health and soil loss. Those picturesque, long lines of crops leave the bare space between rows vulnerable and exposed to wind and rain erosion. And erode the soil does, by the ton. Based on current industrial farming methods in the US, for each pound of food we eat six pounds of topsoil are lost.[3]

Plowing, digging and tilling disturb the mellow balance of bugs, worms, fungi and microbes doing their underground dance. These practices kill the soil's ability to absorb water and prevent the damage wrought by unchecked flooding. They break apart the structure of the soil, which for all time has been layered top-down with mulch, compost, untouched soil and subsoil. The mulch at the top is like a Viking shield for the ground below, percolating water and managing temperatures.

Insects such as earthworms, termites and ants travel through soil and mix it while they do. These critters change the way the dirt is formed in a beautiful, symbiotic dance that is the definition of awesome. Earthworms gobble up soil and other organic residues (food scraps, for example) and as they digest and expel this heady mix, the worms make nutrients more accessible to plants. This all happens while the worm is gently turning soil over, aerating the dirt and making water absorption easy as pie for the soil.

When humans dominate the Earth with a lifestyle too populated and too monolithic to dance in a healthy way — through large-scale farming, compressed city living, gardening in some sterile way depending on bare dirt and chemicals or mowing down open space to put in McMansions, trailers or condos — the system is forced to separate into distinct, toxic groups. And that's precisely when you start running into trouble. For there can be no life without topsoil. So if we don't do something about dirt, we're doomed.

The Septic/Sewer Hoodwink

Humans have taken their own crap and turned it toxic.

All things that grow depend on the waste materials of other organisms in order to thrive. Decaying matter and refuse offer the lifeblood that allows all things to receive nourishment. Dirt — that black gold responsible for all things grown — is the byproduct of decomposition. The earth depends on waste — on poop and dirt — to be healthy. And yet, instead of offering our own humanure waste to the earth in a sane fashion so that it's usable, digestible and capable of being turned into lush soil, we siphon it all away to be treated with chemicals and kept in tanks isolated from all other natural systems.

We take nourishment from soil byproducts — meat and vegetation — then refuse to give nourishment back to the Earth in order to make more soil. We knowingly designed housing in this culture that didn't account for green spaces, which meant there was no hygienic, useful space to store, compost and then use humanure. So human excrement was turned from a healthy addition to the soil structure into a hazardous waste. It has become something to be gotten rid of, flushed away.

We send the stuff from our homes with expensively treated, drinkable water. There are more than 350 million toilets just in the US and almost 320 million people. On average, each American flushes a toilet five times a day. If the majority of toilets use at least five gallons of water per flush, you're looking at more than seven billion gallons of drinking water being flushed into the sewers each and every day. So it's not just that we're ignoring the potential of our own excrement to become dirt. We're adding insult to injury by flushing it with a resource people die without.

Packing all that stuff away means we have huge amounts of too many nutrients and bacteria in one place. Unable to be managed or filtered by natural systems, we are constantly faced with atrocities like so-called sanitary sewage overflows — a nice way of talking about untreated sewage being spewed into nature anytime a sewer line becomes blocked or ruptured, a pumping station malfunctions, there's a human error at a treatment plant or it simply rains a whole lot.

In New York City, experts estimate that more than 27 million gallons of sewage and wastewater land in New York Harbor annually. Many cities like New York have antiquated, underground plumbing systems that struggle to divert epic proportions of rainfall, sewage and industrial wastewater together to facilities for treatments. For the Big Apple, as little as one tenth of one inch of rainfall can cause sewage overflows into city waterways like the Gowanus Canal.[4]

Poorly designed communities and cities historically meant there was no way to deal with excrement; and our nonexistent understanding of germs and bacteria meant festering humanure. That riddled regions with disease. The invention of the flush toilet is credited with quelling rampant outbreak of horrible illnesses like cholera, typhus, dysentery and even the bubonic plague. Queen Victoria ordered piped water throughout Britain — along with treatment plants — after her husband Albert in 1861 died, apparently from typhoid fever.

Dravidians used indoor toilets more than 4,000 years ago in the Indus Valley. Flush toilets were used during the Neolithic Age, and during the Roman Empire toilets were connected to drains that emptied directly into the Tiber River. The first flush-toilet patent was issued in 1775 to one Alexander Cummings.

All of this is well and good, except that culturally we've neglected to improve on the design enough to have a sensible, large-scale way to actually put that poop to good use. And once we stopped pumping sewage directly into the streets or waterways, we resorted to moving the stuff from location to location, dosing it with chemicals, separating it and hoping for the best. But there is so much potential for our poop, it's about time we took a closer look.

The French city Lille and the company GENeco in the United Kingdom utilize buses drawing power from biomethane gas collected out of the cities' treated sewage. Toilets the world over can now break down human waste and turn it into compost and fertilizer. In countries in the developing world, this waste collection can provide an unprecedented boom to agriculture. Millions of homes in China turn methane into power. Designers are working on blueprints for collective waste disposal: low-water toilets flushing waste to shared compost reservoirs that provide fertilizer for gardens and can power an apartment building or several houses with the methane produced. Compost toilets are becoming more mainstream with better holding tanks and more sophisticated designs; on a small scale they can provide private homes with gorgeous dirt all without the use of potable water for flushing crap away.

Waste

Words didn't use to exist for the garbage we talk about today. Trash, litter, garbage: all the terms originally related to compostable materials. But what we think of nowadays as garbage actually refers to waste, which implies something leftover. It implies something that wasn't totally used. It means something to be gotten rid of. And that's an anomaly in the natural world.

How often do you run across a dead body in the wilderness? A dead fly, rabbit, bear, deer, anything? You don't.

Because in nature, there is no waste. Every single thing gets consumed, breaks down, nourishes something else and starts over. We humans are the only living things making stuff that can't break down. Or we use only parts of things and toss the rest. If something breaks, we don't fix it.

Much of what we consider waste is actually food scraps, which we put in plastic bags and send to landfills. According to the US EPA, Americans in 2012 discarded 35 million tons of food into landfills, accounting for almost one fifth of all garbage in the US that year. Waste in landfills is so compacted that oxygen can't reach it so most food scraps never receive the oxygen required for decomposition.

We make things out of plastic that we call disposable. But what does that mean? Think of the energy that goes into making plastic cutlery, the packaging, the money, the sale and the arrangement of that plastic on the picnic table at your next backyard barbecue or on your seat tray during your next airplane ride. How long are you going to use one of those plastic forks for? How long do you spend carrying groceries in plastic bags before you toss them? Is it not completely insane to have stolen so much energy, time and resources to produce something that you are going to use for five minutes and then let it sit in a landfill as waste for the next several thousand years?

There is nothing short of a lack of imagination standing between us and the end of waste as we know it. We have simply neglected to demand a more sensible approach to how we package, manufacture, use and discard things.

The Lawn Lie

The biggest crop in the US isn't corn or potatoes: it's turfgrass.

Perhaps the truest symbol of Suburban America is the picturesque, green lawn surrounding suburbia's pristine houses. Protecting one's lawn has become a civic duty. The wealthiest among us judge our neighbors by their lawns, seeing yards as the red carpet to our homes. But this is a habit, not a need. We gain no nourishment from our lawns. No health benefits. And besides the use of lawns for recreational activities like sports games or picnics, they serve no actual function. But they do cause a whole lot of damage.

More than 800 million gallons of gas are put into lawnmowers in the US each year. Lawns are like biological dead zones offering little to no habitat or food for most species. The US Fish and Wildlife Service reported that American homeowners use up to ten times the amount of pesticides on lawns as farmers use on crops. And Environment and Human Health, Inc., found that almost 80 million pounds of pesticide active ingredients are used on US lawns annually.

The upkeep of these green status symbols is one requiring vigilance, time — and more irrigation than the seven biggest water-sucking agricultural crops combined. The US EPA found that 30–60% of all urban fresh water is used on lawns. And mono-cultured grass in yards needs up to three times the water of a sustainable, mixed landscape.[5]

Lawns don't have to take up so much room. They can be mixed up to include forest, gardens and ponds. They can be grown with native grasses and without chemicals. They can be cut without a bunch of gas-powered mowers and trimmers. What is cut doesn't have to be bagged up and hauled away. It can be left on the lawn to provide protection from the sun, fertilizer for the ground and moisture retention for the soil.

Water

It wasn't too long ago that everyone was responsible for his or her own water. Towns were settled along creeks and rivers. Homes were situated next to springs. Water was carried by hand into the home. That's not easy work. So guess what? Water wasn't wasted.

But we wanted convenience. Now we can turn a handle and water is there lickety-split, hot or cold. Water we use to shower, wash dishes, irrigate our gardens and flush our toilets has been sterilized to be drinkable.

Rivers are rerouted to provide water to farmers, tourism, swimming pools and flower gardens. The amount siphoned off its natural path is divvied up among agriculture (two thirds), industry (one quarter) and residential use (one tenth). Globally, we've dammed up and rerouted with such vigor that many of the world's greatest rivers — the Indus, Colorado and Amu Darya, to name a few — never even reach the sea.

We've created a perfect storm for a massive water shortage worldwide:

1. Our neglect of the soil, which otherwise helps to retain water and provide appropriate irrigation seepage for crops and livestock
2. Our supreme ignorance over what we put into waterways through direct pollution, toxic dumping, runoff and sewage overflow
3. Our neglect of existing water by destroying coral reefs, overfishing, damming up rivers and pulling too much out of waterways for use in desert swimming pools, Big Agriculture and even bottled water
4. Our continued refusal on an international level to truly address climate change and global warming; even as extensive scientific evidence suggests that continued increases of overall temperatures will put natural systems — and humans — at major risk. These consequences include detrimental effects on agricultural production and — you guessed it — rainfall, irrigation capabilities and drastically lowered water tables.

Factor into all this insanity an assumed 70% increase in food demand by 2060, and an estimated 1.8 billion people living without easy access to fresh water.

A satellite analysis in 2014 by NASA found that the majority of groundwater in the world's most important arid and semi-arid aquifers is drying up fast. Water in places like India, the high plains of the US and California's Central Valley is being pumped out much faster than it can be restored. The locations where this is occurring are coincidentally the world's most vital agricultural regions. They're also expected to see the biggest drop-offs in rainfall and soil moisture in response to ongoing carbon pollution.

US Federal authorities in 2001 cut water supply to farming from dams in northern California's rivers in order to protect fish during a drought. The reduction in water resulted in bankruptcies for several Oregon farmers, supporters of whom accused the government of

favoring fish over people. Faced with a similar conundrum in March
of 2002, the federal government chose Plan B and reduced Klamath
River levels in order to provide full water deliveries to irrigators in
spite of a severe drought. People in the Yurok and Hoopa tribes, along
with environmental groups and fishermen, expected catastrophe. But
their multiple requests for increased water flows were refused, and an
emergency release of cold water from California's Central Valley never
came.

So what followed was the largest-known adult salmon die-off in US
history. Salmon washed ashore dead in numbers reaching more than
34,000; though reports indicate this is likely half of the actual number
killed, as many of the bodies floated out to sea or sank to the bottom
of the river.

Tribal communities working together with conservation groups
succeeded in 2013 when the US Department of the Interior recommended the removal of all four dams operating along 300 miles between
Southern Oregon and Northern California and $1 billion in other en-
vironmental restoration.

California leads the United States in reports of drought, yet remains
the leading water supplier for bottled water companies Aquafina,
Crystal Geyser, Arrowhead and Dasani. The companies have to report
what they draw from the groundwater, but have unlimited access to
the tap.

When water rights to the Colorado River were given out in 1928,
Nevada got the least. At that time there were fewer than 90,000 people
in the entire state and Las Vegas was nothing more than a tiny railroad town. The 300,000 acre-feet of water a year (enough to supply
almost double that many families) seemed more than ample. The state
in 2003 exceeded its allotment for the first time in order to serve Las
Vegas' increased number of residents and 65 million tourists visiting
annually.[6]

There are regions all over the world where it is second nature to
have to drill more than a mile to reach groundwater. As more disap-
pears, how will these places be able to avoid violent conflict or human
uprising over this natural resource? How will regional tensions escalate?

Air

Ninety-seven percent of climate scientists agree the rate of climate change documented throughout the 20th century cannot be accounted for by natural occurrences. This one's on us. The buck stops here.

For every mile we drive, we emit on average one pound of carbon dioxide from our vehicles. Power plants burning coal, oil and gas add to the poundage significantly. Deforestation follows suit, releasing more carbon dioxide than all the ships, planes, trains and automobiles worldwide combined. This is something to think about the next time you reach for a paper towel, paper napkin, cardboard cup or giftwrap.

And as bad as the carbon dioxide is, methane's worse. Methane's heat-trapping power in the atmosphere is a full 20 times as strong as carbon dioxide. Yet we continue to make more of it at landfill sites and on farms with large-scale animal excrement and cattle belching. We produce methane every time we drill for oil, frack or mine for coal.

The people pooh-poohing global warming use a harsh winter or heavy snowfall as evidence that our Earth isn't actually on a hot crash course. But there's a big difference between weather and climate. Weather refers to the temperature today. Climate can only be charted by tracking the weather over a long period of time (say, 100 years). Seeing trends over time is what paints a picture of the climate. And that's what's changing — and way too fast to support our lifestyles in the US.

As we drive greenhouse gases like carbon dioxide and methane into the atmosphere, we change the way the Earth's natural greenhouse gases collect the sun's heat before sending it back into space. In short, too much heat gets trapped and raises the overall temperature of the Earth. Even a few degrees of a shift in too short of a time could render the planet unrecognizable. The difference between an ice age and an interglacial period can be as little as 12°F.

In the last several decades, summer sea ice in the Arctic has all but vanished. The South Pole is experiencing large-scale ice melting. Seawater's acidity is up 30% from 40 years ago. The year 2012 was hottest on record in the US. NASA reported in 2014 that a 2,500 square-mile hot spot of methane was hovering over the Four Corners region of the US (where Arizona, Colorado, New Mexico and Utah meet). The gas most likely came from San Juan Basin in New Mexico, North America's most productive coal bed methane basin. NASA researchers estimate that 590,000 metric tons of methane were released from that region annually between 2002 and 2012.

For a long time, we saw air pollution as reversible. Aerosol cans could be done away with, and we could reverse the hole in the ozone. But now, the tide has turned. Unlike acid rain, the influences we are having on the climate are increasingly unmanageable and — more terrifying still — irreversible.

During negotiation of the 2009 Copenhagen Accord, it was agreed upon that 2°C — about 3.6°F — is the extent of a temperature rise our Earth can support without us seeing near-complete devastation of life as we know it now. To stay below that number, scientists figure people can put only 565 more gigatons of carbon dioxide into the atmosphere. Based on our current emission rates, we are expected to reach the 2°C increase by 2028.[7]

If you weren't already depressed, there's five times as much carbon in fossil-fuel industry reserves as is needed to irreversibly tip the scales of climate change. You read that right: We're looking at 2,795 gigatons of carbon sitting in coal and oil gas reserves right now. That's almost five times as much as the internationally agreed upon limit of what this planet can bear. It's already been paid for. You think that's not going to get burned? It would require a major shift in the thinking of our world leaders. And there are only a few ways to get through to them: Money. Supply and demand. Political pressure. Action.

The Intergovernmental Panel on Climate Change (IPCC) said in 2014 that it is still feasible for the planet to stay below a 2°C increase — but it will require scaling back emissions by up to 70% before 2050 and reducing our fossil-fuel use to zero by 2100. Can this be done?

American scientist Ernest Hilgard theorized that hypnosis splits consciousness into two separate components. In a typical experiment, Hilgard hypnotized a subject and told him an ice-cold bucket of water was lukewarm. The subject was told to put his arm in the bucket. Asked how the water felt, the response was consistently that the water felt fine; not cold at all. A paper and pen were given to the individual for writing with his other hand while the first was still in the bucket. The subject was instructed to let his hand holding the pen write freely. The hand wrote, "Take my hand out! It hurts! It's freezing!" Hilgard referred to the second hand as the hidden observer.

We enact this experiment everyday. The mainstream media, fashion magazines, television and Internet hypnotize us into believing change is futile. That we can plug our ears and cover our eyes and continue on without killing each other in the process. That we can buy our way out of the mess and into a nice, relaxed state. But we feel something inside saying this is wrong. This is crazy. This has to stop.

If the ultimate plan is survival, there is no better time to start than now.

Sustainability requires action-oriented decision-making that takes into account the well-being of the land base and all life inhabiting it. Sustainability should reach our agriculture, architecture, economies, politics and homes. This struggle is about values, not just about dirt — but most definitely it's about dirt, too. To adopt sustainability into our everyday lives is a social challenge. On a large scale, it requires lawmakers and politicians to make massive changes in regard to housing, economics, technology and agriculture. On a small scale, there are many things each of us can do to ensure our homes and neighborhoods reduce their strain on the environment.

There's no reason not to make an effort. Until the final moment, there is still time.

Chapter 3

Where I Begin

J une 15, 2009. I was a bundle of raw nerves. Every cell was singing. My belly burned with excitement as my electric-blue Mini Cooper zipped along Route 90 through the highway's Adirondack scar. My palms sweated. I looked across the front seat at Kobayashi Maru, the puppy I'd adopted a few hours into my road trip earlier that afternoon. We Thelma-and-Louise'd our way northwest toward the North Country territory of New York State. The little hairs on my arms tingled. I giggled, momentarily intoxicated by the buzz of question marks waiting out ahead, past the horizon.

Kobayashi Maru mirrored my nervous exhilaration. The goofy great Dane/lab mix eyed me up and down while her tongue lollygagged over her open jaw. She turned her huge Falkor head toward the window and considered the world outside. I reached across the car to scratch the soft, golden fur behind her left ear. The puppy didn't stop panting.

The elation would fade, of course. Random, restless nights would return with quickened heartbeats; second-guesses tugging at the hem of my experience. I would miss the relationship I'd left behind. I'd ache over the uncle who died. I would stress about money and my future, think of friends in New York City padding their 401ks and stock options and wonder whether I'd thrown everything away.

Then those fears, too, would go away.

I clicked on the headlights of the car. Dusk. My 27-year-old self looked out over the highway and disappearing sun. I was headed for the proverbial hills. I smiled.

There is no holy mountain. There is no escape. The only way out is through, though we cower in the face of the unknown. We stay in relationships that don't fulfill us, jobs that don't inspire us and we surround ourselves with people who won't challenge us. We live like our loved ones will never die. We have no urgency. We are trained to fear the unknown. Taught to memorize, not ask questions. Convinced to depend, not create.

I grew up with a glittery vision of turning the mundane magical. My suburban upbringing was stewarded by my parents Laura and Dan, hippies-turned-soccer mom and defense attorney who raised my older sister Kristen and me on Bob Dylan lyrics and classic old movies. We lived in a town neighboring fellow Big Apple suburbs that would one day be featured on "Housewives of New Jersey," protected from the ever-encroaching strip malls and sprawl of the Garden State by a white picket fence that bulwarked our two-acre homestead. Kristen and I ran wild through the property's rolling lawns, tidy bit of woods, gardens, swimming pool, homemade fish pond and large Victorian house. We were a family of card-carrying liberals enjoying upper-middle class privileges. We didn't worry about where our food came from or whether we could drink water from the tap.

My mother and father meticulously instilled a deep respect for the natural world in my sister and me. We were pushed to explore and create, which we did in excess. Kristen and I enjoyed a shared childhood of turned-over rocks, tire swings, soccer matches and tree forts built into the branches of catalpa trees. We played dress-up and made amateur music videos. Family trips were of the cross-country variety, to places like Arches National Park, Grand Canyon, the Redwood Forest, pre-yuppie Martha's Vineyard and Pennsylvania's Amish Country. Sure, we tried on Mickey ears as well; but we were first and foremost lovers of apparently untouched wilds. Our parents grew us to be freethinkers. Over-achievers. Smart. Curious. When I tested their limits and went vegetarian at age nine, it was met with bewildered support instead of resistance.

Relatives on my father's side had a farm a few towns away from where we lived. Kristen and I loved to visit with the emus, pigs and chickens, unwittingly connecting at a young age with how the whole jigsaw puzzle of living things fits somehow perfectly together. During a family trip to Florida when I was barely 14, we stopped one afternoon to visit friends. Strolling through the backyard, Kristen and I discovered hundreds of baby sea turtles. Following a streetlamp instead of the moon after hatching the night before, the tiny animals fell off a low embankment and couldn't get back over to make their way into the ocean. Kristen and I spent the afternoon collecting the tiny reptiles by the skirt- and armload and casting them back into the sea.

One of my favorite places to visit was my dad's brother Steve's commune in Northern New York; it was called Better Farm. It had served since 1970 as a stopping ground for members of the back-to-the-land movement, hippies, dropouts, visionaries and adventure-seekers alike. Even my parents, whom I had trouble imagining as free-spirited kids, lived there as newlyweds the first summer Steve owned it.

Spending time at Better Farm, a full day's drive from my suburban home, was like visiting another world. There were no rules. Stacks of springy old mattresses served as beds while scraps of fabric functioned as curtains. Chairs with sawed-off legs were floor seats outside. The place had pigs living in the barn across the street (with a pot-bellied one in the house for good measure), children skateboarding up half-pipes in the driveway, chess games in the kitchen and acre after acre of woods and fields to explore. The place was a living, breathing vessel that held decades of family history, endlessly good ghosts and a voluminous body of stories with no shortage of people to tell them. I was in love. As I grew into a teenager, annual pilgrimages to Better Farm became monthly activities shepherded by my father and attended by as many friends as I could squeeze into the backseat.

My dad died in 1999 from a massive heart attack. The suddenness of this loss gave me an unnerving sense of urgency and ambition. In the ensuing years I grew obsessed with travel and spent every summer during college seeing the US by bus. I left nothing unsaid. I stopped watching TV. And I started visiting Better Farm regularly on my own.

I considered myself a truth-seeker. Planning to one day find my way onto the masthead of *National Geographic,* I earned two secondary journalism degrees out of high school, cut my teeth first at a weekly newspaper then as editor-in-chief of a major magazine and plowed ambitiously into the working world of journalism. My articles appeared in several high-level magazines and trade publications. I was interviewed on Fox News and in the *New York Times.*

Those years were rich, for sure. But in spite of my nearly feverish travel resume — four cross-country trips by bus, two stints in Europe, several forays into South America and a handful of Canadian and Caribbean adventures all before I'd turned 25 — I grew unmotivated by my own, everyday life.

By 2006, the year I licked grad school and earned the distinction of being editor at an internationally known glossy, I'd acquired the habit of spending at least a half-dozen weekends each year at Better Farm. Once there, in a sleepy little hamlet time forgot, I felt my heart rate slow and anxiety subside. The rushed stress of city life left me. Sitting at the kitchen table with my Uncle Steve working on *New York Times* crossword puzzles, taking solitary hikes in zero degree weather through property he'd since donated to a local nature conservancy, sitting on the back deck watching the birds: Better Farm felt like home to me. And though the head count had dwindled since the house's wild 70s era of rebellious gardening and multi-colored house paint, the aura was still there.

My uncle and I daydreamed about what it might be like to revive the space. Could we pull artists from the city who might find inspiration at the farm? Could we put in gardens and work the land? Was there a way to combine the two? We talked renewable energies like geothermal and solar. We imagined artist residencies and educational programs. We pictured art and music festivals where people could share ideas and inspiration against a creative, green background. A better way for a yet another generation hungry for more than the ever-disappointing status quo.

I'd return to the city each time, too chicken to make a move. I felt trapped at my desk.

In 2008 I was hired as editor-in-chief of an elite trade publication covering the New York City diamond trade. Despite my utter disdain for the diamond industry in general and a keen distaste for corporate America, I was grateful to land the job when the gig I had savored lifted print issues temporarily in favor of an online template.

Six months in, I felt old: a woman without a cause who worked for a paycheck instead of a passion. I got up early, took a combination of subways to work, sat in my cubicle all day while listening to people around me discuss TV shows from the night before, took the reverse route home, went for a jog, made dinner, and lay in bed reading until I fell asleep, exhausted. It was no way to live — though I knew all along this was exactly what most people do.

Working overtime in a cramped cubicle space took its toll — and fast. Gone were the long-distance bus trips. So long to hitchhiking, jaywalking, honky-tonking and kootchy-kooing. I was too tired to keep up with my *Finnegans Wake* book discussion group. The bicycle I stored in my apartment collected dust. Even the spinach plants I labored to grow on my windowsill looked ill. I'd arrived at adulthood; and though I laughed every day and was seen as a free spirit, inside I felt myself disappearing.

In January of 2009 my Uncle Steve, then 67, contracted a bad case of pneumonia. While I frantically communicated from New York City with doctors in Arizona where Steve had been wintering, I felt him slipping away. I took time off work and flew to Tucson to see him. The stress of Steve's illness and the growing realization he might not recover put added pressure on an already tumultuous, two-year relationship I had been embroiled in. Unable to cope, I broke up with my boyfriend and started seeing a shrink. A week after the break-up in March of that year, Steve passed away.

Then I got laid off. That was the last straw.

I blinked back tears that early afternoon as I climbed into a subway car in Manhattan with my arms full of reporters' notebooks, a dicta-phone, a handful of pens and my Rolodex. I felt embarrassed. A failure. Back in my apartment, I sat on the couch and stared at the wall of bookshelves. There was no one to call. Nothing to figure out. I raised the metaphorical white flag and took off my high heels. I shuttered the windows of my mind and invited my pain in for tea. There was no need to open my computer. No crying. No yelling. Just numbness.

I moped for days. The self-pity was suffocating.

I began looking for work the following week. I applied for hundreds of editing and writing jobs, signed up for unemployment, and tried to keep my head above water. I got small writing gigs but no big bites for full-time work. I grew panicked about money.

To compound these issues was an additional detail: Uncle Steve left me Better Farm. I knew that was coming, but hadn't expected to be 27 and unemployed when this transfer of property came to be. How would I support a huge house on 65 acres six hours away when I couldn't even pay my rent?

Without steady work and desperately in need of distractions, I began volunteering in a community garden in the Bronx. I tended compost bins and planted flowers in the mulch and dirt of the Big Apple and cried the whole way there and back. I made a concerted effort to spend more time outside. I started a vermicompost bin under my kitchen sink. I went to parks and ate cucumber sandwiches and sat outside coffee shops with my laptop.

I had trouble sleeping. I tossed and turned while fretting over what to do with Better Farm. I thought about renting the house out. Using it as a summer place for family and friends. As time passed, I also entertained the dusty old fantasy of trading New York City for Redwood. I imagined having a writing career outside of a cubicle. And I pictured doing with Better Farm what I'd always dreamed. But the idea of giving up on so many so-called real-world goals in exchange for life in the country seemed too enormous, too frightening, to even consider.

Months went by. One evening in May I rode a crosstown bus back from a friend's apartment feeling particularly pathetic and sad, silently reciting all the usual, pessimistic anxieties I'd grown so used to. But then something else happened. Out of nowhere, a new realization hit me like a sucker punch from the divine. Maybe it was my subconscious finally yelling "Scene!" Maybe it was all the gardening. Maybe it was sheer exhaustion. I felt my skin turn to goosebumps as new ideas came in torrents; synapses exploding like fireworks in some weird, beautiful grand finale. The world isn't out to get me. Eureka! Losing a loved one doesn't set me apart. Amen! I am not defined by my job status or relationship. Yum! I'm not stuck. Aha! My life can look however I want it to.

Better Farm was my uncle's Hail Mary pass. I was meant to catch it.

Just like that, the butterflies left my tummy. I stopped crying. And finally, something started to shift.

From that moment on, I knew I was bound for motion. The match was lit. The fat lady had sung. The cows had come home, and the pigs could fly. I heard the unmistakable sound of ice forming in Hell. Over all that commotion, other voices told me not to throw away the master's degree I'd worked so hard for. Suggested I'd never meet someone to marry in such a small town. Told me I'd be giving up, shuttering myself away, checking out. Told me I shouldn't go so far away from everyone I know and love.

I kept packing anyway.

Less than three months after losing my uncle, job and boyfriend, I adjusted my sails. Armed with a hands-on version of the Better Theory and an ingrained interest in environmentalism and art, I pointed my car northwest, adopted a puppy and headed straight for Better Farm.

Chapter 4

Better Business Practice

W<small>E ARE LIVING THROUGH AN ERA OF RECORD POPULATION</small> that ironically coincides with record isolation. Our jobs, along with our addictions to social media and television, exacerbate this issue. We have an "Every Man for Himself" mentality in the dominant culture of the US that encourages us to go it alone — either truly on our own or as an independent family structure. We treat our shopping experiences, jobs and neighborhoods as separate pieces further distinguished as somehow apart from our personal lives. In our isolation, we gobble up resources faster than they can be replenished. All our independent activities and enterprises have added up: On a global scale, our expenses (natural resource use) surpass our incomes (how quickly resources can be renewed in nature) by 150%.[1]

For humans' place in this world to be more sustainable, more loving and more fulfilling, we have to change how we do business on Planet Earth. Let's stop pretending that we're not connected to the businesses we patronize in the communities where we live. And let's not forget that the businesses we patronize must also do their part to live in agreement with the landscape.

What if we stopped justifying our apathy and instead demanded that business ethics mirror the ethics we want our children to learn? What if we insisted the developers making our neighborhoods took the environment into consideration? What if our communities were extensions of ourselves that we played an active role in shaping and supporting?

All this might bridge the divides we have. It might help us feel connected. And it just might heal so many of the social ills that plague us.

Involvement isn't so far-fetched. Time and again we have seen businesses spring up founded on morals, ethics, philanthropy and environmental empathy. There are ways to poke through a seemingly universally corrupt system. To choose love over greed and to make it work. Business owners, entrepreneurs and start-ups all over the world have begun a new trend of corporate community and environmental engagement that enhance the venture's relationship to the neighborhood in which it is based.

No small part of the disconnect we experience stems from our limited relationships with our communities and local businesses. Examining how businesses can be fused with their neighborhoods offers insights into ways we might all become more actively engaged with our local economies, shopping habits and environments. The glue connecting all these points is a shared vision of a better life for business owners, consumers, children, neighbors, friends and even the landscape.

Sustainability in any setting must first and foremost take the local environment into account. What businesses and communities in Northern New York do to be more sustainable will differ significantly from counterparts in New Mexico, Bangkok or Newfoundland. Local ecology should dictate the methodology, materials and design of businesses located therein. How we interact, care for, take from and nurture the natural world around us must adhere to the local land base.

To identify the needs of a community, you have to put your feet to the pavement. It is only by listening to people's stories, experiencing the sights, sounds and smells of a place and breathing the same air that we can empathize with a space, person or landscape. Smart entrepreneurs know that analyzing data alone won't make them innovators; instead, they know to bury themselves in the questions of how they can improve upon life in their communities in a way that also speaks to their business models.

In 2001, University of Illinois researchers France Kuo and Bill Sullivan conducted a study to compare the lives of women living in a Chicago housing development. Half of the test subjects lived in apartment buildings with views of greenery. The other half lived in identical buildings without those green views. Kuo and Sullivan found that buildings with high levels of vegetation outside had 48% fewer crimes against property, 56% fewer violent crimes and less domestic violence.

Of 200 residents interviewed, 14% of women with barren views reported hitting their children in the last year. Only 3% of women in green areas said the same. Similarly, women enjoying views of trees outside reported fewer violent acts toward their partners than those living without trees. Residents living with green views also demonstrated better relationships with their neighbors: more visitors, more socialization, more knowledge of who's who and a stronger sense of community.[2]

Developers armed with such research findings can fundamentally change social dynamics among residents in their communities. Imagine marketing houses and apartments with proven abilities to reduce crime, isolation, depression and violence.

When our corporate ventures or organizations grow out of a community's needs, our mission becomes part of a higher power and larger body of work. When this happens, employees and customers alike are drawn to the vision. We see things firsthand and experience all that life offers to us. We open ourselves up to our communities and each other.

There isn't any reason for business practices to be separate from neighborhood outreach. A vibrant and successful small business will incorporate a community's identity into its very core. If a business owner can envision a better community and have a carefully orchestrated action plan for facilitating change, then there is a strong relationship that will allow for regeneration and evolution.

To establish itself within a community, a company must assess its neighborhood's needs and file those down to efforts that merge business practices with the community. A farm may wish to donate to the local food pantry, while an office-supply store may give school supplies to local children. Smart collaboration is more important than a misguided laundry list of things a neighborhood needs.

Bennu, a green product development and marketing company focused on recycling, organizes an annual "Greenpacks for Great Kids" online backpack drive. The company donates $5,000 worth of eco-friendly backpacks to children living in low-income, New York City communities.

Vermont-based Bove's Cafe and pasta sauce company partnered with Hannaford Supermarket to donate 1,000 boxes of pasta and more than 1,000 jars of pasta sauce to the Chittenden County Emergency Food Shelf. Bove's took what it knows how to do — feed people — and used that skill to help the community.

Bob's Red Mill Natural Foods founders Bob and Charlee Moore in 2011 donated $5 million to Oregon State University in order to establish a research center focused on the nutritional value of whole-grain foods. Another $1.35 million was donated by the couple to the National College of Natural Medicine as help in the fight against childhood obesity.

Maple Leaf Adventures, a boutique expedition company based out of Victoria, British Columbia, annually donates one percent or more of sales to coastal conservation work and science. These funds have supported the prevention of illegal trophy hunting of grizzly bears, research on seabirds and white spirit bears and helped to protect wild Pacific salmon. Each of these causes is near and dear to the hearts of the company's owners; Maple Leaf Adventures relies on this coastal environment for ecotourism.[3]

Communities demonstrate needs through certain indicators. How do people handle their garbage or treat their front lawns? Is the local school struggling? Is natural landscape incorporated into the scenery or banished from it? Are children playing? Are public spaces tidy? Are there any public spaces at all? It's easy enough to explore an area by researching basic information about the local economy, housing, environmental degradation or bounty, topography, transportation, public health and basic demographics. But so much can be learned by actually entering the environment: hike, kayak, walk the trails and explore the old railroad tracks.

This is the beginning. But we have to look even closer, at the canvas behind the neighborhood.

The land that's supporting businesses and homes is the backdrop to all we do within it. When creating a business model, we are wise to consider the land and what it can realistically support. We must consider the people who depend on that land whether they realize it or not. This is not some fall-by-the-wayside topic; it's everything. How can my business support the local land base? How can my company help to clean up the local ecosystem or establish conservation efforts? How can my office produce zero waste? How can I use renewable resources to power, heat and cool the buildings I use? How does my presence in this location enhance the natural landscape that makes it possible for me to live and work here?

Companies should not continue to produce things that hurt either the environment or community. Enough technology and information is accessible now for us not to need things like genetically selective weed killers or toxic toilet bowl cleaners. There is no longer any excuse to use polystyrene foam containers, paper towels or paper napkins. The boom in small farms and the technology we have to communicate with each other leave little excuse for our restaurants not to incorporate local ingredients. Our office kitchenettes don't need throwaway cups or plastic stir straws. There's no reason to buy these products, offer them up for employee use, and there's no reason to sell them. It's unconscionable to not compost food scraps when we know how beneficial they can be. We can start companies that don't create products that harm the land base. We can appeal to the companies we work for to green their practices.

As consumers, we have power. We increase or decrease demand by buying or not buying. This is the only language many companies know. If we all stopped buying paper towels or factory-farmed meat, what business owner in her right mind would continue to try to sell them?

People utilized social media in 2010 to create a massive campaign against Nestlé for its use of Indonesian palm oil in its products. Initially launched by Greenpeace, the Facebook-driven campaign provided information on how demand for palm oil in Indonesia spurred growers there to illegally cut down endangered rainforests in order to make more growing space for palm. A petition was passed around, but consumers got in on the game directly by writing their own letters to Nestlé and posting on the company's own social media sites about the issue. Consumer action went viral throughout the Internet, and Nestlé responded with a pledge to source 100% of its palm oil from certified-sustainable sources by 2015. It met that pledge a full two years early, in 2013.[4]

Visitors to Sea World locations in the US dropped by 13% in the first quarter of 2015,[5] following the release of the controversial documentary "Blackfish." The film, which outlines a number of violent outbursts of whales against their trainers, explores the complex intelligence of killer whales and suggests the mammals are unfit for captivity. Public outcry against the theme park resulted in free-falls for Sea World's numbers. Stocks fell 50% in six months during 2013, and the park's CEO resigned in early 2015.[6] The dramatic drop in ticket sales has meant a scramble for Sea World execs to rebrand the company and to put an onus on rehabilitation and education over tricks and captivity.

A 2005 McKinsey & Company study found that up to 8% of consumers had stopped shopping at Walmart because of negative press about the company's environmental practices, labor policies and methods for beating out competition.[7] In response, that same year Walmart's CEO announced a sustainability strategy that would allow the company to in the near future "be supplied 100 percent by renewable energy; to create zero waste; and to sell products that sustain our resources and the environment."[8]

We are alive during some of the most exciting times. A huge majority of the people creating start-ups want to make a positive contribution to the world. And luckily for them, a business model that incorporates philanthropy is infinitely more attractive to investors. Courageous leaders who insist on higher standards are rewarded tenfold by consumers.

Actor Paul Newman launched Newman's Own in 1982 by passing out wine bottles filled with homemade salad dressing to his friends. In the three decades since, the company has earned more than $400 million — all of which has been donated. Every after-tax dollar earned by the company goes directly to Newman's Own Foundation, which distributes the cash throughout the world to various charities.

Newman's has inspired countless other corporations to follow suit. Mike Hannigan, one such company's founder, had his moment of reckoning while reading over his own jar of Newman's pasta sauce. Hannigan got in touch with his business partner and the two men figured out a way to instill philanthropy into the core of their venture, Give Something Back Office Supplies.

Though it's a mega-chain, Chipotle is another great example of business practices being intertwined with community outreach and sensible principles. The corporation buys as much as possible from local farms within striking range of each franchise. Chipotle selects farms that are informed by their local land bases and utilize compassionate care for livestock.

Life is good, Inc. makes a ton of money selling merchandise depicting its now-famous stick figure emblem. The company has built charitable giving directly into its business plan, donating 10% of net profits to children in need. Life is good also sponsors festivals that give merchandise and profits to child-related charities and causes.

Since 1985 outdoor gear biz Patagonia has donated one percent of annual sales to environmental causes and preservation. But they've done more than that: in 2013, the company unveiled a new campaign called "The Responsible Economy." This effort is to produce fewer items than in previous years and limit growth in order to put less stress on the environment. Patagonia's high-quality outdoor products are designed to ensure consumers can wear the same gear year after year. The company is single-handedly challenging the compulsive clothing shopping experience other businesses depend on.[9]

The more a community understands an organization's positioning, the better the relationship will be. So aligning a business with one or two specific causes will benefit business owners and employees more than token contributions. This work doesn't have to be money-based, either. Any community will show more respect for business owners who get their hands dirty helping out with neighborhood cleanups or fish fries than some mogul who throws money at community issues.

Virgin Group founder Richard Branson is a billionaire who devotes most of his time to philanthropy. His chief effort is Virgin Unite, a nonprofit foundation with projects related to leadership and entrepreneurship. Branson has said in many interviews that healthy profits are inextricably linked to community support of a business's services and management practices — and that employees want to work for businesses they believe in.[10]

Steve Brockman, locally celebrated business owner of Expert Plumbing in Naperville, Illinois, regularly rolls his sleeves up to help his community. He works closely with Naperville Western DuPage Special Recreation Association, and has in the past built a parade float and organized a fundraiser for the group.[11] And senior staff at Solihull Hospital in the UK annually show their appreciation to the rest of the staff by contributing during the hospital's National Volunteers' Week. Pitching in unpaid in the pharmacy department, meeting and greeting or helping with fundraising efforts are the higher-ups' way of saying thank you to the people who put in the elbow grease every day to make the hospital run smoothly.[12]

Notre Dame High School in Clarksburg, West Virginia, launched a new initiative in 2015 called "Business Gives Back." For that program, area business owners visit the school to talk with students about making a difference in the community and the benefits of local businesses offering volunteer outreach.[13]

There is growing evidence that our happiness is actually tied to local economy and policy. The Gross National Happiness (GNH) movement, started in Bhutan, factors happiness into new policies. A commission in that country reviews policy decisions, distribution of resources and studies the effect of these factors on the level of happiness within the country. Similar to environmental impact measures, governments that use GNH indexing adjust their policies according to the levels of happiness those policies will bring to communities.

Factors include the environment, culture, art, physical and mental health and basics like economics. So now, it's possible to chart how a government (in its own right an extension of a company profile) affects the well-being of the communities it is supposed to serve. It's a model worth considering in our own households, civic centers, states and counties.

When we seek business ventures that solely satisfy our greediest, most egocentric concerns, we limit ourselves. We feed an addiction to material gains and a hectic life that leaves us exhausted and unfulfilled. Living in this way only expands our sense of being alone. But opting for community-driven business practices enhances neighborhoods, increases happiness levels and is good for businesses' bottom lines.

Chapter 5

Building a Better Farm

*Better Farm is a 65-acre sustainability education center,
artists' colony and organic farm nestled in the foothills
of the Adirondacks and Thousand Islands Region.
The property was founded in 1970 on the principles of the
Better Theory — a belief that every experience brings with
it an opportunity for exponential personal growth. Through
educational workshops, artist residencies, sustainability programming and an ongoing commitment to green living and
community outreach, we at Better Farm strive to apply the
Better Theory to all our endeavors while offering the curious
an opportunity to expand, grow and flourish.*

Better Farm, 1970.
CREDIT: CALDWELL FAMILY

THE FIRST-RECORDED SURVEY of what would become Better Farm was made November 10, 1890, by one J.H. Scott, ten years after the little farmhouse was built. Farming couple Alfred Davis and his wife Vaughn bought the 150-acre property in 1955 from the Felder family, though it would continue to be called "the Felder place" by locals. Alfred had spent his childhood in Morristown about 20 miles north of Redwood and, in addition to running their homestead, picked up a job in 1966 at Tibbles Lumber Company in Redwood.

The couple had five sons and would eventually be blessed with 13 grandchildren. Then in 1970, disaster struck.

That winter 60-year old Alfred fell ill. A neighbor, Frederick House (who some say befitted his name by being truly as large as a house), came over on January 8 to look after the ailing Alfred while Vaughn drove the family car into Redwood in search of medical help. Upon her return, however, Vaughn found Alfred and Frederick both dead in the master bedroom. Medical Examiner Jay W. Edison was called to the scene and filed a report listing cause of death for both men as heart attacks.

Vaughn put the farm up for sale that spring.

Meanwhile 350 miles away, Stephen F. Caldwell was hot on the trail of a new life.

Seven years earlier, in 1963, Steve completed his undergraduate work at Columbia University in New York City. The 21-year-old tennis star and promising student planned in the fall to begin work as a reporter at *The Record,* a regional daily newspaper in New Jersey where his father and uncle served as editors.

The universe had other plans.

Three months after his graduation, Steve was on a cross-country trip with a young woman named Janet whom he'd dated during college. The two had been at a Sunday screening of "Ben Hur" but left the film early to begin the long drive home. Steve sprawled out across a bench seat in the back of the Volkswagen van to sleep while Janet steered. The vehicle motored along the black line of Route 40 about 15 miles west of Wendover, Nevada, as Janet fell asleep behind the wheel. Neither passenger wore a seatbelt. When the van rolled over into a wash along the shoulder of the road, Steve was thrown from the vehicle. Janet's body landed eight inches from the left front wheel of the car. She was killed instantly.

Hours passed.

A truck driver saw the wreckage and pulled his rig over. He found Steve, dragged his broken body to bring him closer to the road and radioed for assistance. "Chicago Woman Killed in 1-Car Mishap Sunday," the *Elko Daily Free Press* would report. "Stephen Caldwell, 21 . . . was seriously injured and is being treated at the Elko General Hospital."

Steve's diagnosis was spinal cord injury resulting in quadriplegia; all four limbs suffered varying degrees of paralysis. He had total numbness and loss of voluntary control from his armpits to his toes, save for spasms of phantom pain. He could move his arms but had lost his ability to grasp and hold with his hands. Multiple surgeries attempted to restore manual dexterity in Steve's hands by transferring tendons from working muscles to tendons of paralyzed muscles. The surgeries worked: Steve thereafter could grab a short peg with which to tap keys on a typewriter, hold a fork or grab the handle of a mug by making a pinching motion between thumb and hand.

Steve was moved in June of 1964 from rehab at Columbia Presbyterian Hospital in New York City to join siblings Cath, Bob and Dan and parents Mary and Bob at the family's Victorian home in Ridgewood, New Jersey. For the next seven years Steve would live in two large rooms that comprised half the ground floor of his family's house. He used a manual wheelchair he could barely move himself, slept in a hospital bed and, except for numerous trips to and from hospitals, was out of doors fewer than six times a year. He was often, unsurprisingly, miserable.

When in his wheelchair, Steve sometimes sat in front of his Selectric typewriter. He wrote hundreds of reviews which were published in the *New York Times, Psychology Today* and the *Saturday Review of Literature.* His poems were printed in various literary magazines.

Steve in 1965 started playing poker in a game that included a rotating cast of family members and friends. The group gathered most Friday nights in Steve's room to play poker and talk. The Friday-night gatherings eventually waned and by 1970 had ended.

The conversation, however, did not.

The Caldwell Family, 1967. Clockwise from bottom center: Steve, Mary, Bob, Robert, Cath and Dan. CREDIT: CALDWELL FAMILY

The Summer of Love had come and gone. Steve had survived dozens of surgeries, been in and out of hospitals on a regular basis, and had it up to here with living as an invalid in the downstairs of his parents' house. So when he received insurance money for his car accident, the 28-year-old decided to buy property elsewhere and invite his friends to live there communally.

His brother Dan, then just 21, got hold of a Stout Realty catalogue in March of 1970 and found a farm listed with a house, barn, milk shed and garage just a few miles from the Canadian border. He and his friend TJ hopped a small plane from Teterboro, New Jersey, to Watertown, New York, where a real estate agent picked the young men up at the tiny airport and drove them the remaining 25 miles into Redwood.

"We walked around the place, thinking this is about as basic as we would want and that with some work it would be alright," TJ recalled.

Downtown Redwood, New York, 1970. Credit: Caldwell Family

By the time the realtor returned from getting coffee in town, Dan and TJ said they'd take it.

"We thought the kitchen with the hand pump was unique and the small space heater in the house was adequate — we had no idea how cold it got that far north," TJ said. "There was no insulation — more like a wind deterrent than walls." The house had no indoor plumbing, only one electrical outlet in each bedroom and a potbelly stove in the kitchen whose stovepipe ran through the ceiling to the hall upstairs and then outside.

To the uninitiated boys from Jersey, the place was perfect.

Steve signed the deed in May of 1970 from one Vaughn Davis for the total sum of $10,000 and named the property Better Farm. Better Farm lore is that Vaughn took the money and hired herself a personal driver for the rest of her days.

That first summer, more than a dozen people stayed at the farm and began the process of converting it into a space appropriate for Steve;

complete with eventual indoor plumbing, wheelchair ramps, more extensive electric and a small vegetable garden. TJ and his Army buddy Bob Hillegass were the only two well-versed in construction, but others proved eager to learn. Plans were drawn up to double the size of the house and build the first floor of an addition entirely out of stone. Lumber would be purchased at Tibbles, the same lumber company where the farm's previous owner, Alfred Davis, had worked before his untimely demise.

"It was really hard work that summer," Steve's cousin Bill Caldwell remembered. "It wasn't just a hippie commune but a major construction site." The workers waked at 6 AM, devoured a breakfast of oatmeal and coffee and piled into Hillegass's green 1950 Ford pickup truck to go out and collect rocks for the addition's foundation. "Some of those rocks weighed like 200 pounds," Bill said. "It took three or four of us to pick them up, load them into the truck, bring them back to the farm, unload and repeat. One of the guys living at Better Farm refused to do physical work. He built a plastic greenhouse in the yard and spent all day there. That didn't sit too well with the troops."

Not everyone agreed that an addition was necessary, either. "I was unenthusiastic about that, as it seemed to me that we fit pretty well into the house as it was," said CB Bassity, who arrived at Better Farm during the first summer and would be back throughout the 1970s, even wintering alone there in 1973. "Enlarging the place was just bringing our suburban, consumerist lifestyle to a place that could do without it."

Bob Bowser, who got to Better Farm that June, had been in a car accident in March and was unable to contribute physically to the construction project on the house. "I mainly worked in the kitchen doing dishes and making 20 pounds of potato salad every other day," he said.

Bill Caldwell, 1970. CREDIT: CALDWELL FAMILY

"I did contribute $1,500 from my own insurance settlement, which Steve paid back with interest in the 1980s."

At the end of each day's work, everyone from the farm went two miles down the road to Millsite Lake to wash off. "Everyone swam stark naked," Bill said.

"Boys in the town liked watching the nude hippie chicks swimming in the lake," TJ said. "There was quite a group of spectators. People in town used to drive out to the farm to see the hippies on a Sunday afternoon."

"They stared at us as if we were a zoo exhibit," CB added.

But for all the exoticism and fun, politics of communal living got in the way for a lot of people — many of whom had conflicting reasons for being at Better Farm.

"The term 'better,' as I remember it, was used ironically," CB said. "If you had a flat tire, or the lumber yard shipped the wrong material, or something similar, you'd say 'Better.'"

Bob Bowser stands at the site of Better Farm's addition, 1970. Credit: Caldwell Family

"It took my first six weeks there to get the foundation basically ready and then we faced the prospect of building all the rest of the addition from stone," Bill said. "Those of us with calendars in our brains said, 'This ain't gonna be done in time for Steve to move in this fall.'" The realization drove a rift between the work crew, and TJ soon left. "The rest of us were suddenly alone there with no one with more than an eighth-grade wood shop education in construction," Bill said. "It felt like we were the crew of 'Mutiny on the Bounty,' although I didn't look much like Marlon Brando."

Steve's brother Bob came to the rescue, arriving in Redwood with his friend Dick Groat; they supervised the construction of a wooden addition for the house atop the stone foundation. By late July there was an indoor toilet and shower. "To be able to use all the facilities of a modern bathroom felt like an incredible luxury," Bill said. "I remember people taking half-hour hot showers."

Bowser called the first incarnation of Better Farm a "social experiment with a bit of *Lord of the Flies* and a bit of 'Survivor' and some from a few of the great social psychologist experimenters." He referenced Phil Zimbardo, who conducted the Stanford Prison Experiment, and Muzafer Sherif who did the Robbers Cave Experiment on kids at a summer camp to study competitive and cooperative scenarios.

"Beyond the goal of preparing the house for all of us to live in when Steve came in the fall," Bowser said, "there was no common vision of what we wanted the farm to look like. Some wanted it to be very rustic with no indoor plumbing or hot water or furnace. There was no clear leadership so it was leadership by the strongest personality. There was no sense of how the farm would be sustained or governed. We all agreed that we wanted to live communally, enlarge the house, and that we all enjoyed drugs and music. We agreed on little else."

Better Farm would provide the symbiotic albeit imperfect web of relationships Steve needed to live an independent life. Able-bodied people could do the cooking, cleaning, building, chores and physical routines he couldn't. Steve could help pay basic expenses and utilities at the house with the modest income he earned from occasional writing gigs and being on permanent disability.

*Work crews
build an addition
to the small
farmhouse in
1970.*
CREDIT:
CALDWELL FAMILY

Steve moved to Better Farm that October, thinking he would live there permanently. It proved otherwise. He was back and forth between Ridgewood and Redwood until, in 1973, he first wintered in Tucson, Arizona. Thereafter he split his time between Redwood and Tucson. While he was away, Better Farm stayed occupied with people committed to his vision of intentional and shared living.

"The Better Farm story of 1970 is the story of about 16 young people," Bowser said. "They were mostly from affluent families, mostly cocktail party radicals — Steve subscribed to the *The Black Panther,* the Panther Party newspaper — who hung out together around Steve in New Jersey and who decided it would be cool to take Steve's settlement and make a commune."

But caring for Steve was no short order. There were catheters to contend with, bowel routines every few days, the often daunting task of getting him in and out of bed and monitoring him for fevers that might belie other conditions he couldn't feel. Untrained friends and occasionally nurses who made calls at the farm or happened to live there carried out these jobs and many others.

Most days, Steve parked himself at a folding card table and recorded stories on an old typewriter that would evolve into a half-dozen short novels and many volumes of poetry. Steve became a beacon of resiliency who inspired many of the people who lived with him to go on to pursue careers in nursing, counseling and community outreach. The people in his surrounding solar system were, in his words, "invigorated by my perverse joy of life." He taught others acceptance and love by the openness he dared to share. He gave his heart away: everything he learned, his modesty, his ability to say no. He was vulnerable. He loved people who couldn't love him, he fell for women whose hearts belonged to other people. He was a constant in a sea of change. And because he knew he was powerless, he possessed great power.

There's a choice each of us makes after a tragedy: will this tragedy own me, or will I own this tragedy? Plenty of people in this world choose to wear their pain like a badge. They use their hardships as excuses to be hurtful to one another and leverage their pain as currency. Steve saw tragedy as its own currency, a way of paying him in increments of sorrow in order to enlighten his joy. Steve made a choice. Roundabout, yes. Selfish, maybe at times. But he made a choice nonetheless to not allow a physical limitation to force him into bitterness. He taught, and loved, and learned and created a space that is so holy and sacred that people who have no concept of that history enter it and feel a sense of belonging.

That is Better.

Steve considered himself radically agnostic, saying: "For me, suspension of disbelief is a useful, even necessary, exercise." He used that suspension of disbelief to propel himself into an extremely active lifestyle; including daily bird-watching trips that occasionally totaled up to 17 miles at a clip in his automatic wheelchair. Steve's independence awed the medical profession, and his repeated brushes with illness and death seemed only to embolden and inspire him.

For the residents of Redwood who'd spent the better part of a century with very little outside influence, what was called "the hippie farm" became a bull's-eye on the North Country map. Stories are still told of topless gardeners, epic parties and the various attempts by the people living at the farm to actually work the land.

"Given the era," CB said, "and that we were long-haired kids from elsewhere wearing tie-dyed shirts and so on, I wondered if there were folks in town who had it in for us. For the most part, however, we were just accepted. A friend who moved to the area a year or two later also remarked that he was so impressed by the tolerance of local folks — it's why he settled there — when the cultural divide was so fraught in other parts of the country."

With time, the wilds of Better Farm faded. The restless teenagers paired up, married off, settled down and moved away. They had restless teenagers of their own. The war in Vietnam ended. The mantra "Don't trust anyone over 30" lost its effect as the people reciting it surpassed 30, then 40 and 50. The whole world revolved out there as people aged and sold out and got distracted by their jobs and earthly responsibilities. Steve stayed behind, a time capsule of a hopeful generation without form.

My arrival in 2009 at the farm didn't coincide with a business plan. I let Better Farm grow out its own history, the neighborhood

Better Farm dwellers outside the main house in 1979. Steve Caldwell is seated at far right. Credit: Better Farm Archive

surrounding it and the people who visited. Today's incarnation of Better Farm would be nothing without a close relationship to its local community and the artists, students, movers and shakers who shape it.

During that first year, my sister helped me build a website and start a limited liability company (LLC) while friends acted as my IT, marketing and education departments. By the spring of 2010 I was ready to go public, so I contacted my alma maters Hampshire College and Columbia University, along with a handful of other colleges, to let them know there was a new experiment underway. I explained that Better Farm would be offering a hands-on education in sustainability initiatives in units like compost, permaculture, mulch gardening, small livestock care, aquaponics and more.

That first summer, 2010, several students, artists, musicians and gluttons for the unknown got in touch to say they wanted in on the fun. Jackie, Joe, Tiyi, Ali, Corinne, Butch, Colleen, Mark, Eric, Purwin,

Brian, Clayton, Chris and Sarah all showed up to set the proverbial ball in motion. Struggles ensued, all worthwhile, that further refined my direction and educated my ideals about this project.

From there, the wind was at my back. I fine-tuned the application process, renovated several more rooms, expanded the gardens and hammered out a curriculum that allowed students to design their own areas of focus. Each year Better Farm's offerings have grown to answer needs presented by the people who live here. Each year the projects change. Each year we sell to the public more and more organic produce that is cheaper and fresher than what they can buy in a store. And every time someone leaves, so too does he or she leave something behind: a

Better Farm Today.
CREDIT:
NICOLE CALDWELL

building she helped construct, a mural he painted on a wall, a tree she planted. In this way the history of Better Farm makes new history. The walls, should they ever talk, will have a whole lot to say.

There are many differences between incarnations of Better Farm. In its beginnings, waves of young adults from the Tri-State area arrived by van, bus or thumb to get away at Better Farm. But today, the space is a training ground for people who will return home with new skillsets and perspectives to share with the world. What was once a liberation from the status quo has embedded itself in North Country culture. The farm can't function if it doesn't give back to the region in some way.

So it does. Better Farm hosts festivals that explore the intersection of sustainability and art. Volunteers from Better Farm participate in Earth Day cleanups and run booths at science fairs. People staying at the farm welcome anyone who would like to stop in unannounced to sit on the front porch and talk. Strangers welcome each other and learn and teach and even heal in this way.

Better Farm is no longer an escape. Sure, people still find it refreshing — a nice change of pace from their city or suburban lives. But Better Farm is completely attached to the towns and counties around it. The farm's entire focus is on educating and inspiring people so they can leave and make differences back home.

The central concepts that educated Better Farm's business model have grown and expanded. The venue now also houses betterArts, a nonprofit offering artist residencies, workshops, festivals, community support and even a radio station: WBTS 88.5 FM, Better Radio.

Better Farm is dedicated to small changes and ripple effects. Redwood businesses and homes boast compost systems where there weren't any, and the hamlet now has its own community compost system and greenhouse in addition to its preexisting community gardens. People living locally who might not be interested in sustainability have front-row seats to the farm's initiatives through events and everyday conversation. The Redwood area is now home to at least a half-dozen new residents who were drawn in whole or in part by Better Farm. People who have stayed at the farm have gone out into the world and made things Better.

Better Farm Dwellers, 2011. CREDIT: ERIN FULTON

Sally Jane Kerschen-Sheppard waked one day in New York City and found that she was 35 years old. "It felt like a deadline," she said. "I had four part-time jobs, all of which were steady but with no growth potential. Yes, I was paying the bills. Yes, I had health insurance. Yes, I loved living in New York City. But I was stagnant, and I decided that I could either live exactly this way for the rest of my life, or I could change it. So I changed."

Sally Jane — an award-winning playwright, certified yoga instructor, production manager for theatre events and worker in the not-for-profit sector — came to Better Farm through the betterArts Residency Program in August 2012 to work on a play she was writing. She also helped in the gardens, cared for — and rescued from an egg factory — dozens of chickens, and provided home cooking to everyone staying in the house.

"Living at Better Farm for a month inspired me to take the things that made me the happiest and try to make them part of my everyday life," she said. "I had worked for nine years at a summer writers conference, and I loved being surrounded by my fellow writers and all that creative energy. So instead of only having that experience once a year, I decided to start my own writers residence in Detroit so that I could have that creative energy all year round."

She put a bid on a five-bedroom house up for a HUD auction in Detroit and got it. Sally Jane moved to Detroit by herself, readied the house for artists-in-residence, named it Blue Field Writers House, and posted an application form online.

"The process has certainly not been easy," she said, "but I know if I were still in New York right now, still stagnating, I would be miserable. For me, it was better to take the risky leap than to not leap at all. Everyone I've met in Detroit is thrilled that I moved here, that I started Blue Field Writers House and that I'm helping to build a strong literary community. There is a sense of excitement here because the potential for creation — a new business, a new piece of art, a new community — is so palpable. Visiting writers can't help but feel that potential for themselves, and every one of them has commented on

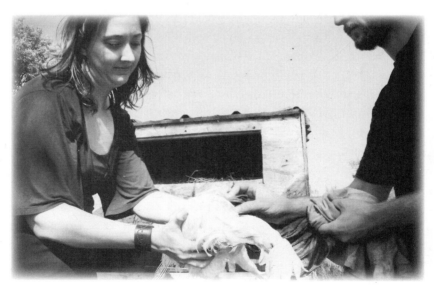

Sally Jane Kerschen-Sheppard (left) and Matt Smith rehabilitate chickens just rescued from a nearby egg farm in 2012. Credit: Nicole Caldwell

how inspired they are by the city. Detroit is on the cusp on something big, and I am delighted to get in on the ground floor."

Kathryn Mollica arrived at Better Farm in 2013 as a sustainability student. She was just shy of getting her undergraduate degree and had been working part-time at an organic supermarket. She came into her own at Better Farm, learning to assert herself, be a leader and get her hands dirty. She opted to stay on an extra month, went home and accelerated her graduation, got promoted at work and returned the following summer as Better Farm's Director of Education and Farming. By the end of that summer she'd put the groundwork in place to start her own bakery company (aptly called Mollica) that features organic, locally grown ingredients.

Kathryn Mollica harvests fruits and veggies at Better Farm, 2013.
CREDIT: NICOLE CALDWELL

Elizabeth Musoke grew up in Kenya and moved to the United States to study at the College of Architecture, Planning and Design at Kansas State University. She came to Better Farm in 2011 as a sustainability student. Her interest? To learn about rainwater catchment systems as potential for providing water-supply solutions to people back home who lacked a steady supply.

"I was really interested in innovative ways to encourage water reuse and conservation," Lizzi said. At Better Farm, she designed and constructed a gutter-based rainwater catchment system that provided basic irrigation to one acre of gardens and fresh water for the chickens living

Sustainability students Elizabeth Musoke, Jaci Collins and Soon Kai Poh build a garden gate in 2011.
CREDIT: MARK HUYSER

on the property. After her stay at Better Farm, she pursued a PhD at Kansas State researching water quality and soil erosion in Kenya. "I miss Better Farm," she said. "Until this day I am still telling people about my experience there and the wonderful people I met."

While Better Farm may not be able to stop industrial waste before the planet is too sick to take on all us humans, or reverse global warming, or change governmental policy, we can continue to push for changes and make our own. We can stop ourselves from feeding into a system that is the polar opposite of sustainable. Making hundreds of tiny decisions every day to reduce our footprint, improve the soil in our backyards and keep as much as possible out of landfills, greedy corporate pockets, waterways and even the air, then these small things done at home will become big steps toward getting back in line with what nature intended.

Which is to say we might lend ourselves a bit more to infinity and improve the natural life cycles all around us that we've lost so much sight of.

Better Farm Dwellers, 2013. CREDIT: ERIN FULTON

Chapter 6

Where Sustainability and Art Intersect

T HE INTERSECTION OF SUSTAINABILITY AND ART is the intersection
of the heart and the mind. It is the synthesis of everything dear:
fundamental survival, connectedness to the natural world, beauty,
truth and love.

A child plays with an upright piano growing produce out of its top. The piano was donated to Better Farm, played until it was beyond repair, and then repurposed as a planter and ongoing group mural.
CREDIT: HOLLY BONAME

Art came before language. It is the most integral part of our humanness and demonstrates time and again our perspectives on humanity's
place in the world. As soon as we could pick up a rock we were etch-
ing in caves about our relationships with god, with animals, with each
other and with the world around us.

Science alone isn't enough to stir the souls and minds of many. The
Earth is complex. Multi-layered. Rich. There isn't a straight approach to
fully include all the vastness of the world. To understand the depth of
the planet — and to counter the environmental and spiritual problems
we face in today's world — we're going to need creative, collaborative,
fun, cultural advances. This is a job for the arts. Art piques our curiosity, which invites debate and discussion. From there, it is only a matter
of time before we arrive at new ideas and solve problems in new ways.

Science is about facts — but the science of sustainability also involves
values-based questioning. This is where art comes in. Governments
and cultures worldwide have acknowledged the need for sustainable
development and varying methods to deal with climate change and
environmental degradation. If we can acknowledge the power of art
to transform society and the world, to bring magic back into our lives,

Using dead leaves as stamps, we call attention to where paper comes from.
CREDIT: NICOLE CALDWELL

then we allow art to become a catalyst for change where the scientific method falls short.

Think of how timeless pieces — the Mona Lisa, the Sistine Chapel, Warhol's famous soup can — have instilled wonder in people. If art can inspire cathedrals, the pyramids and the entire marketing world of the 21st century, just think of how art can alter people's perceptions of sustainability. If apathy among the public is adding insult to environmental injuries, then the best way to facilitate change is by exciting the public enough to raise a ruckus.

The implications for art intersecting with sustainability are huge. Each of us possesses an unbelievably powerful tool that can change the world. Tons of new art is coming out that's been produced sustainably with natural, eco-friendly materials. There is art with a sustainable message. There are seed bombs. There is upcycling. We need the radical, innovative platforms that only art can provide to communicate between governments, cultures, communities and individuals. Art may be our strongest weapon in battling the daunting environmental issues we face. It offers clues to creative answers for some of the world's most difficult questions.

Dutch artist Daan Roosegaarde collaborated with Heijmans Infrastructure to memorialize Vincent Van Gogh with a solar-powered bike path illuminating an interpretation of Van Gogh's famous Starry Night painting. The installation was done in Nuenen, the Netherlands, where Van Gogh once lived.

Eve Mosher's project called "Seeding the City" involved placing trays of growing plants on 1,000 rooftops in New York City. Each of the participating buildings was outfitted with flags on roofs and at street level. Mosher's intention was to elevate the conversation about ways to clean and cool the environment. The flags, along with the participation of building owners, drew visibility to this project.[1]

At Better Farm, projects exploring where art and earth overlap come up on a regular basis. An old toilet destined for the dump was turned into a planter on the property. A friend living locally teamed up with a resident to turn old 50-gallon metal drums and tire rims into a metalworking forge. And each spring, those staying at Better Farm run

"The Doors" series by artist-in-residence Mike Brown involved installing discarded, brightly painted doors into dead tree trunks on the Better Farm property.
CREDIT: NICOLE CALDWELL

Visitors to a memorial festival in 2010 come together to paint doors for "The Doors" series. CREDIT: NICOLE CALDWELL

workshops with children to make biodegradable planters for seeds that, once plants take root, go directly into the soil.

The growing sustainable art movement is spreading. Sustainability has already been institutionalized into elective concentrations at a number of art schools; thereby allowing students to mesh their creative processes with ecological issues. Programs like these pull art into the larger societal context and allow artwork to address real-world problems as they apply to the environment.

A more sustainable, loving future for this planet is sure to only rise out of a richly diverse cultural movement that pushes new ideas and perspectives into the public eye. Art is the captain able to steer that

During a renovation project at Better Farm, an old sink was turned into a planter instead of thrown out.
CREDIT:
NICOLE CALDWELL

ship, with work realizing fresh ideas and alternative realities. As lobby groups, protests and governing bodies point fingers and criticize the status quo, art has the ability to suggest new ways of being and envision a greater future. A more sustainable world relies on the shared responsibility of government, culture, communities, the arts and the individual.

Sustainably minded art projects are great not because they fix a problem at hand altogether, but because they encourage people to think about the problem. They acknowledge there is something in dire need of our attention. The wonderful thing about art that addresses sustainability is that it's limitless. Sustainability doesn't have a specific look. No real style will encapsulate it.

When you talk to children about the benefits of growing their own food, and you give them biodegradable seedling trays they can then decorate, paint and handle, then those kids can become stewards of the earth, raising seeds up into small plants and then putting them in the soil outside (maybe with some compost they've helped create).

A child decorates a biodegradable planter; he will then put organic seeds in it. When the seedlings are ready to go in the ground, the boy will put the whole thing — planter and all — into the Earth. This activity nurtures creativity while teaching children about plant science, compost and soil.

CREDIT: NICOLE CALDWELL

Through an art activity the young artists can attach real meaning to the sustainable act of gardening. Instead of believing we are beyond hope, through art making we can explore ways to contribute to new global visions that promote sustainability, love and community.

When you upcycle a piece of trash and turn it into art — or better yet, functional art — you're showing everyone around you what power creativity has: power to keep trash from landfills, to inform, to influence, to inspire and to bring more beauty into the world.

To make art, we are required to determine creative ways to deal with problems and questions, and to engage with the public. Artists ask questions like: How can I invoke empathy? In what way will this piece affect people? They do their research. They analyze their findings through art.

Art has the power to make people think and connect. Individuals who study the arts are more likely to be recognized for academic achievement, be elected to class office and score higher on the Scholastic Aptitude Tests. Students who study art are less likely to be

Sustainability student Jaci Collins in 2011 created this piece of art out of an old window, leaves she found on the ground and some paint. CREDIT: NICOLE CALDWELL

involved with drugs; those who were in band or orchestra report the lowest lifetime and current use of all substances.

Art promotes mindfulness and fights stress. Creating art puts the maker in a meditative-like state, disengaged from problems in the exterior world. People with ADHD report being able to paint for hours. Studies demonstrate art's ability to improve body image, reduce levels of the stress hormone cortisol and ease symptoms of depression.

Art is healing. It boosts immune function, reduces depression, and alleviates pain. Creating art amplifies self-confidence, improves brain function, and has even been used to aid individuals recovering from addiction.

Research shows improvements in expression, reduced stress, and increased positivity for those who take up a creative hobby such as painting or writing, or who decide to pick up an instrument. In a study published in the *Journal of Psychosomatic Medicine,* writing was used as a treatment for HIV patients. The result? The act of writing actually improved patients' immune systems. Dance or other movement-based creative outlets improve motor activity, reduce stress and promote better circulation and flexibility overall. Music therapy has been used to reduce anxiety, boost the immune system and stop chronic pain. Art is one of the most classic ways psychologists and social workers communicate with children who have dealt with trauma; art therapy has proven to be an integral tool for adults dealing with life-threatening health diagnoses to reduce their depression, anxiety and pain.[2]

Arts and culture funding has a great return on investment. Low-income high schoolers who are educated in the arts are more than three times as likely to earn a BA as low-income students without arts training — which means lower costs in welfare and incarceration, and more taxable income. For each dollar the city of Toronto puts into arts organizations, more than $17 is pumped back into the economy from private and public sources. ArtsServe Michigan found that in 2009, every $1 the state invested in arts and cultural groups brought with it a return of $51 through rent, salaries, tourism and programming. And Americans for the Arts reports a 7:1 return on investment for every dollar the three branches of federal government annually put toward arts and culture. These statistics are food for thought as deficits continue to soar and we debate how to use public funds most efficiently.[3]

When we bring the arts into our community outreach work, we are building more vibrant neighborhoods across generations and demographics. Art engages people who might otherwise feel apathetic toward being active in their community.

It's time we stopped allocating art to two distinct, far-fetched worlds: that of highbrow fine artists with pieces hanging in museums — and the doodles of children. To see art in these ways — as entertainment, as childish, as luxury or extracurricular and unnecessary — is a crime. Art is a portal into our most basic instincts and desires. It is healing, it is freeing, and it is soothing.

It is the connection between our environment and us. And it's going to be a big part of how we get out of the mess we're in.

Better Farm's garden sign, painted on an old bunk bed headboard by visiting WWOOFERs Mollie Mahon Cross-Cole and Sarah Hawkins. Credit: Nicole Caldwell

Chapter 7

betterArts

betterArts is a nonprofit organization offering access to creative exploration and growth to artists of all kinds within the context of Better Farm's dynamic environment. betterArts is dedicated to expanding cultural and creative opportunities of the rural North Country by offering year-round artist residencies, art and music lessons, studio space and cultural events for people living locally and beyond.

betterArts volunteers in 2013 set up this canvas at a local crafts festival for children of all ages to help decorate. CREDIT: NICOLE CALDWELL

T HE CONCEPT OF ART IMITATING LIFE — in fact, noting that art has been central to our humanity since people first stood upright — became evermore obvious the longer I lived at Better Farm and worked

betterArts members volunteer at the 2014 Better Festival held at Better Farm. CREDIT: BETTER FARM ARCHIVES

Visiting artist Kiran Chandra works in the library at Better Farm in 2014.
CREDIT: NICOLE CALDWELL

on so many literal things: cultivating food in the gardens, building structures with my hands, harvesting rainwater. I began to notice a trend in the visitors to Better Farm. By and large they all took on creative ambitions during their time here. There was a lot of art being made seemingly all the time — and often not by people who considered themselves to be artists or even artistic. Movie nights turned into face-painting marathons and collage parties. Broken tiles became mosaic tabletops. Bedrooms got murals, stones and chicken feathers became jewelry and impromptu photo shoots sprang up all over the property.

Visitors, students and friends who stayed here said without pressure, without cable TV and with arts supplies on hand, being creative came very naturally. Many people who hadn't painted in years were suddenly dipping brushes into bright buckets and decorating walls, paper and wood. Out-of-practice potters began shaping clay and using a kiln at a local studio down the street to fire their pieces. Artistic creation became part of everyday life at the farm. Volunteers from Better Farm started attending community events and hanging canvases for group murals, leading upcycling projects and helping children paint pumpkins.

But it wasn't just novices, either. People who studied art, lived and breathed art and taught art started to get in touch. The sustainability studies being pursued at Better Farm were the exact backdrop they sought as they created. Writers wanted to be surrounded by gardens while they wrote their novels and plays. Painters wanted to take breaks from their easels to help pull weeds or feed chickens. Glockenspiel players, guitarists, drummers and singers wanted to tend aquaponics tanks or take the compost bucket out before sitting down for several hours to practice. These things somehow went together.

It was becoming obvious to everyone that the more we connected with the Earth and each other, the more attuned we became to our creative instincts. So a residency program was established in 2010 that invited artists to visit Better Farm for a week, a month or longer to work on a series of paintings, collection of poetry, sculpture or new media project. A few friends helped me design a basic application packet, and out it went.

By 2011 it was clear this program had a life of its own so several people got together to create a nonprofit specific to the arts and culture outreach coming out of the farm. betterArts is now a 501(c)3 charity organization focused on expanding cultural opportunities. No longer just for artist retreats, the nonprofit leases space on Better Farm's campus for gallery openings, festivals, concerts, workshops in everything from weaving to violin lessons, volunteer work in the community and all sorts of public exercises in creativity.

The betterArts board of directors is comprised of a retired Army vet, former television reporter, bookkeeper, boat builder, licensed psychologist and many more individuals representing the diversity of North Country characters. The nonprofit is housed in a converted barn on the Better Farm property that is used for concerts, festivals, gallery shows and studio space. And through every betterArts initiative — each workshop, free concert, artist residency and community mural — sustainability lies at its heart.

Better Farm functions to empower people to make more sustainable, creative decisions in their daily lives. betterArts' role is to examine where sustainability and art intersect — and how art can be used to impress upon people the dire circumstances we're in.

What Better Farm and betterArts endeavor to teach, in essence, is the power of single steps. These two organizations suggest that these steps are necessary; even if the power of art alone isn't going to make a politician change course or mean that we suddenly lose interest in the oil reserves of the Middle East, Canada or dear old Alaska.

Because each step toward sustainability does matter to that earthworm and to this body and to all the tiny life systems affected by every square foot of healthy compost. It matters to every single organic vegetable and responsibly raised animal. And these steps walk us away from a linear, consumerist culture that celebrates what's disposable and deplores all that lasts. Sustainability matters to that one person affected by a piece of art — and it matters to the person who picks up that dusty guitar after years away.

And if each of us can get one drinking buddy or grandmother or coworker to realize that small difference, maybe he or she or they will start doing something small, too. And with all those small things come bigger things, come all the other important things needed to bring about that very large change that is really so completely necessary.

Better Farm provides people with a living laboratory to test out sustainable ideas. People visit for a night, a month, two months or an entire season and spend their days figuring out green systems for everyday life. They've outfitted a small cabin with a solar kit, researched, designed and installed several rainwater catchment systems, built greywater filters, constructed multiple outbuildings, put together compost toilets, studied companion planting and employed it in our gardens and utilized a no-till, mulch-gardening system that relies on biodegradable matter, natural pesticides and fertilizers.

Artists, visiting through the betterArts Residency Program, have given Better Farm's sustainability mission a voice that soars. But conceiving the residency program wasn't enough on its own to satisfy all the needs of artists; they needed physical space, too. So while Kate wrote poetry in an old school bus on the property and Mike practiced glockenspiel in the library, in 2011 I started renovating the barn across the street. The second story was filled floor-to-ceiling with hay, while

Eric Drasin in 2009 plays drums in Better Farm's unrenovated barn.
CREDIT:
NICOLE CALDWELL

the first floor was overflowing with random catchall items from the last 20 or so years. Tricycles, plastic sleds, lumber and bagged clothing covered the floor and rose toward the ceiling in the corners. I gave away or used all I could. Anything beyond repair or recycling went into a

The betterArts Gallery. CREDIT: NICOLE CALDWELL

The betterArts Studio. CREDIT: NICOLE CALDWELL

dumpster. Friends came over and helped to cut out windows on the front and back of the barn to let some light in.

The first floor got swept out, plywood walls were installed, and everything got painted white. Rows of track lighting set the stage for a gallery space; the cathedral ceilings and metal roof on the second floor created a rustic, wide-open studio.

An outside staircase made getting to the second floor simpler than climbing an interior ladder. And when finished, the second-floor deck made for a perfect stage overlooking a natural amphitheater. Thereafter, all events held at Better Farm revolved around the newly renovated Art Barn.

In addition to the bounty of undisturbed forest and landscape, food grown on-site, a rotating cast of characters to bounce ideas off of and curate shows with, betterArts residents now had their own big studio space. And with all these tools to complement their overwhelming talent, betterArts residents have moved the Better message out beyond the

betterArts Art Barn and Amphitheater. CREDIT: BETTER FARM ARCHIVES

betterArts resident Kevin Carr's sculpture work. Kevin used discarded bottle caps and bread ties to make large, 3-D pieces drawing attention to how all the little things we throw out cumulatively become enormous. CREDIT: NICOLE CALDWELL

farm without a single argument or picket sign. They've educated the public — and themselves — through their art.

"A lot of my work is about collections of objects that are often over-looked because they appear insignificant," Kevin Carr explained, "but when displayed in large masses they become significant and make people think about what the object really is, what it does and why it is so small." During his betterArts residency, Kevin researched the average amount of plastic shopping bags a family of four goes through in a year. Then he collected that amount of used grocery bags, cut them into strips and made a series of knotted roped to demonstrate how much waste this amounts to. He also collected discarded bread ties and bottle caps to create large-scale sculptural pieces outside that intensified the striking difference between natural and manufactured.

"For a while, I had wanted to create works involving recycled items," Kevin said, "things that would normally be thrown away or tossed somewhere to sit forever. Imagine thousands of beer bottle caps, bread clips, plastic grocery bags or discarded receipts shown or displayed to-gether in a systematic way. This would draw the viewer's attention to how throwing away something small like a rubber band or a toilet paper tube can actually cause a large amount of waste when 15 million other people each just threw away one of these objects."

Visiting artist Lilli Fisher came to Better Farm because she wanted to explore relationships between humans and the environment. Lilli worked on temporary installations featuring living and decaying items that created habitats, were consumed or were constructed by organisms in the ecosystem.

"My work is a physical process of searching in which I investigate my existence in the context of contemporary life," Lilli said. "I collect discarded human-made objects before they are swallowed back into the earth. I gather waste from industrial production and daily con-sumption. My aim is to provide a sensual experience, removed from the boundaries of language, which encourages the viewer to question his or her paradigms. During my betterArts residency I wanted to gain a personal understanding of human-ecosystem interactions through organic farming and create pieces that are integrated into the living fabric of their environment. I also wanted to take advantage of valuable feedback from the Better Farm community."

For her gallery exhibit at Better Farm, Lilli made three-dimensional sculptures out of invasive flora and fauna in the North Country.

betterArts resident Lilli Fisher made giant, temporary sculptures entirely out of invasive species. At top, "Moving North" is created out of locust pods; at bottom, a spider-like burdock sculpture measuring more than six feet long rises off the Art Barn floor.

CREDIT: LILLI FISHER

A huge burdock sculpture hulked in a corner of the Art Barn gallery while black locust pods appeared as a giant tangle climbing up off the floor. Lilli also made a time-lapse photography project of Better Farm's chickens eating suet cakes she made and shaped into letters spelling the word WILD.

betterArts Resident
Kareema Bee.
Credit: Better Farm Archives

Artist-in-residence Maggie Fishman created a series of drawings and paintings that would later be built into a book called *The End of Oil*. The pieces explored how common stories and themes shared by humanity are acted out in a world we are told is near its end.

Poet and filmmaker Kareema Bee created a video montage of her time at the Farm, accompanied by poetry:

> I saw the wind blow differently here
> with a sort of fearlessness I had not known
> not whimsical or absent-minded but
> with a sort of entitled dysfunction
> I guess you could say homegrown
> Clucks as loud as trucks that wind roads with no curves
> and heartbeats dedicated to string guitars and running
>   herds
> of smiles that greet you
> and crimson throats that swallow hard times of turmoil
>   bourbon
> lethal.
> This little town with its carnival lights and dancing paws
> riveting waves and humble quarters
> some say even distant dreams on island waters
> I remarkably found fun
> I felt free
> I found a better start
> a better purpose
> a Better Farm
> and a better me

Sculptor Natalie Collette Wood came to the betterArts Residency Program to explore the relationship between abstraction, identity and the virtual era. "In an age of rapidly growing technology, war and natural disasters," Natalie said, "our environment and identity have begun to change before our eyes. I am interested in the sublime moment when things start to fall apart and structure and chaos dance. My collages use abstraction, the landscape and personal experience to create a visual diary." For her final exhibit held at Better Farm, Natalie hung sculptures from the ceilings and walls that she created out of found objects, wire, iridescent paint and wood. "My sculptures have been a continuation of my exploration into the relationship between abstraction and the virtual age," she said.

Part of the requirement in the betterArts Residency Program is community outreach. To that end, artists must contribute time in Better Farm's gardens, on other projects or volunteering in the community. betterArts has hosted dozens of free workshops utilizing upcycled

betterArts board member Matthew Tardif decorates pumpkins with children at a local school. CREDIT: NICOLE CALDWELL

Visiting violinist Brian Purwin picks string beans in the garden at Better Farm. CREDIT: NICOLE CALDWELL

betterArts resident John Dunsö came from Sweden for a residency while he worked on his new album. The singer-songwriter loved caring for the chickens during his time at the farm. CREDIT: NICOLE CALDWELL

materials to make instruments and art — like kazoos from ice pop sticks and caterpillars from egg cartons. Volunteers from the nonprofit have taught children how to make dyes from berries, print in paint with leaves, and they have used discarded scraps of mat board as canvases for pictures of children's favorite vegetables.

All this work meant momentum. News channels started doing segments on visiting artists. Radio stations made mention of our sustainability and art festivals. Artists-in-residence gained visibility in local and regional newspapers. I became a regular guest speaker at the local community college, and business magazines profiled the organizational structure of Better Farm and betterArts. Every community event in the North Country wanted betterArts reps there doing sustainable arts projects with visitors.

betterArts acquired an ever-expanding platform of art and increasingly diverse set of voices. So when news arrived that the FCC was taking applications for low-power FM stations throughout New York State, betterArts jumped on the bandwagon. Better Radio was approved in 2013 and is designed to promote the people, art and ecology of the North Country.

That station, in conjunction with betterArts' website, provides content to people living locally on-air and worldwide via podcasts, live streaming and sound files. Better Radio is set up to broadcast talk shows, live and prerecorded music, interviews, storytelling, news, weather, fishing reports, poetry, garden guides and anything else the station's volunteers can dream up.

Part of the work of Better Radio has been youth involvement. Grant funds were used for New Media training for teenagers in the North Country. Volunteers acquired recording equipment and work with young adults in a variety of disciplines to educate them on principles of recording, uploading, syncing, mixing, digitally editing, creating podcasts and producing content in a way that draws attention to the community.

All this programming is meant to push the Better message forward. A person doesn't visit Better Farm and then go back to life as it was. People go home with the skills to start a community garden, grow salad greens or hook up a small solar kit. They fix things instead of throwing them out; they are creative every day; they reuse and refurbish. They host art installations centered on sustainability. Their work inspires other people. And all these small, beautiful actions are spread from person to person, fanning out from place to place and inspiring a symphony of change.

Walter Dutcher (left) and Carl Frizzell install Better Radio's tower on the Better Farm property. CREDIT: NICOLE CALDWELL

Part 2

Above all, watch with glittering eyes the
whole world around you, because the
greatest secrets are always hidden in the
most unlikely places. Those who don't
believe in magic will never find it.

— Roald Dahl, *Charlie and the Chocolate Factory*

Your vision will become clear only
when you look into your heart.
Who looks outside, dreams.
Who looks inside, awakens.

— Carl Jung

And the day came when the risk to remain
tight in a bud was more painful than the
risk it took to blossom.

— Anaïs Nin

Chapter 8

Where You Begin

YOU DO NOT NEED TO LIVE IN DENIAL in order to have the semblance of a good life.

This is your moment, though maybe you don't quite know it yet.

You've reached a crossroads. You can stay the course on the road you're on — or you can take what you're learning and do something with it. You can be destroyed by the hand life dealt you, or you can let it embolden you. Where will your life be in ten years — if you stay the same? If you change?

This is the tipping point. Which way do you want to go? Will our futures be dictated by nine-to-five jobs, bottom lines, uncontrollable circumstance and fossil fuels — or by sustainable love, energy, autonomy and natural systems? We already have the technology, know-how and resources to reduce our carbon footprints without surrendering all of the things we're accustomed to. We don't have to give up vehicles, shopping, a climate-controlled home or convenient access to food. In fact, we can make changes that will save money, offer more security and make us happier and healthier.

The changes we can make one at a time will create jobs. Allow us to live richer lives. And promise our children a brighter future. It all starts with one mindful step in which we ask how our decisive actions affect ourselves, our neighbors and our planet.

Awareness comes before choice. The Better Theory functions by pushing us to practice awareness that is naturally followed by acceptance, then action toward living our best lives. By using this approach we connect to a higher power — one more in rhythm with our own needs and the needs of the world around us. When we work through things that are difficult, we maximize our ability to find a sense of purpose and meaning. We learn more about ourselves. We are humbled by reaching out for help. Through this process, our pain becomes our teacher, and detriments become aides. We have effectively transformed the negative into a positive.

When we see the environment around us as an extension of ourselves, suddenly where our food comes from is of the utmost importance. It's simple to start a small garden at home even in a very limited space, and to supplement homegrown produce at farmers markets and with locally sourced food. Growing our own provides us with food security and safety, nourishes the dirt, drastically cuts our carbon footprint, creates circular loop systems, saves money, boosts biodiversity, relieves stress and makes us healthier.

We are more prone to a divine sense of oneness when we live this way. We experience the exhilaration of standing at the edge of the Grand Canyon or looking at the stars through a telescope. We are one tiny part of a greater whole. Everything doesn't depend on us, and yet our actions interact with and influence other actions. We are free.

In so recognizing the interconnectedness we all share, we make the first steps toward living a more sustainable and loving existence. No action occurs in a vacuum. Spending time in a garden produces spiritual awareness. The creative process can help us foster a deeper respect for the natural world. All these elements combine to give us a sense of our wholeness.

The only way to close the gap between people and planet is to make new connections. And when we can tap into the Earth, connect with each other and our selves, fear dissolves. This work can start with you.

Maybe you hate your job and would love to do something different — but you have a mortgage/six children/a spouse who doesn't work/thousands of dollars in credit card debt. You have debilitating physical ailments, and you just want to give up. Your relationship with your girlfriend is unfulfilling, but you don't want to be alone. You have an idea for a new business, but what if you fail? You don't have time to garden. Or you don't know how. Getting your family to compost seems impossible. All this green-living stuff is at best an exercise in futility. You were never any good at art — and anyway, who has time for that?

Jennifer Fink is a 36-year-old from York, Pennsylvania, whose sister Jackie attended the betterArts Residency Program in 2010 for pottery. When asked about her own creative outlets, Jennifer had this to say: "I used to take solace and pride in my work and now all that has kind of died. I just get frustrated when I try to write or do art. I would need more time to dedicate to fixing that part of me than I would have available, I'm afraid. To me, being a responsible adult has been nothing more than the massacre of all my hopes and dreams for myself. I need to figure out how to enjoy art again."[1]

Sound familiar?

We have caused unknown damage to ourselves by creating a world that compartmentalizes vocations: logical people versus ethereal; people who work with their hands versus those who sit at a desk; work versus play; form versus art. When is the last time you used your hands to make something? The last time you felt dirt on your skin, or cooked something from scratch? When is the last time you doodled or took a pottery class? Think about what this act of creating means to you and ask yourself why you don't do it so much anymore.

The high aspirations that dominated the imagination of people in North America in the 1950s now permeate our culture. When trying to identify the American Dream today, we still commonly think of owning our own house, having kids, convenience, material accumulation, leisure time, status, career mobility, security and continuing education. While almost all of these traits are luxuries or perks, our society has come to see them as tools required for survival in today's world.

The sense that we must achieve this huge laundry list of standards in order to somehow be okay is garbage. And it's making us — and our planet — very sick. Seventy percent of Americans are on prescription drugs, according to a 2013 Mayo Clinic report. The second-most common prescription among these was for antidepressants.[2] We've got the blues. Is it such a mystery why, when so much of our focus is on the achievement of or attention to unnecessary things that we perceive as necessary?

Millions of people have struggles similar to yours. So many of us are paralyzed by our own fear of the unknown and a worry about what might go wrong if we try something different. Fear breeds paralysis. It feeds off of itself. It pushes dreams and compassion out the window and takes up all the room in your head. We become aware of our own dissatisfaction but do little or nothing to accept and change it. We are dealt mental and physical blows in this life that seem insurmountable.

"As we speak, I am recovering from a spinal fusion," said Kelly Rouba-Boyd, a professional writer and newlywed who was diagnosed at the age of two with juvenile rheumatoid arthritis. "Aside from having to stay in the ICU once before due to internal bleeding, this has been one of the most difficult times in my life. It's also not how I had hoped to begin my life as a married woman. To be honest, I wasn't sure I'd make it to my first wedding anniversary since my doctor admitted it was a very dangerous surgery.

"But here I am, still going strong. The human race is extremely resilient. When faced with adversity, we often find ways to overcome it — and that is exactly how I've chosen to live my life. The disease has taken quite a toll on my body, and I am reliant on a wheelchair to get around. But I never let grass grow under my wheels. I believe in pushing past limits and making the most out of the life we've been given." In the last several years, Kelly authored a book on juvenile arthritis, was named Ms. Wheelchair New Jersey and was honored with a $100,000 annual juvenile arthritis research grant named after her. If Kelly can do all of this, certainly we can get over a crummy breakup. Surely we can cultivate a garden. Of course we can compost.

"When a longtime friend saw the long scar that now runs down my entire neck," Kelly said, "it surprised me that he didn't wince. Instead, he said it's symbolic as it shows others how tough I am. I hope my efforts have inspired others to live life to the fullest — no matter what hand they've been dealt."[3]

The challenges we face as individuals, communities, governments and as a whole planet are also huge opportunities. Let's not overwhelm ourselves. Let's start small. If you can make a few small changes, a ripple effect will take hold for you — and for the people around you. There are ways to jump from the treadmill we're on. There are ways to slow our lives down enough to actually enjoy them. If you can practice Better and treat your problems as opportunities, your experiences will improve. And when your friends and family see your transformation, they're likely to start making some small changes too. And the power of that small change, spread out across the world, turns ripples into tidal waves.

It begins with you. You have to change your thinking; change how you look at the world. Seek magic. Find coincidence. Practice wabi-sabi, the art of finding beauty in that which is unusual or incomplete. Heed your inner voice. Suspend your disbelief. Stop saying no, yuck and can't. Start saying yes, yum and can.

Former betterArts resident Jennifer Elizabeth Crone has always been interested in making the world better for people experiencing homelessness. So it wasn't unusual when in 2014 she went out on her birthday, bought a bunch of bagels and then handed them out to homeless people on her walk home from yoga. But that day, something changed.

"I was so gratified by the experience of giving them out and the short but powerful exchanges I had with the people I gave them to," Jennifer said. "I thought about how I wanted to do more and help more people, but the task always seemed so incredibly daunting."

Instead of letting the feeling pass, Jennifer did her research. She found out that her San Diego community has the largest population of homeless veterans in the United States. She learned that the fastest growing population of homeless people is children under nine. So Jennifer posted an event on Facebook and invited her friends to join her in feeding 50 people living on the streets and then go out and have brunch together — "My idea of a pretty awesome Sunday," Jennifer said. She stayed up late that Saturday night writing notes of encouragement to be handed out along with the food. Sunday morning, six people showed up at Jennifer's house. The troupe made 60 peanut butter and jelly sandwiches, bagged the food up with toothbrushes, granola bars, bottles of water, socks and the notes, and handed the packages out to homeless people.

"I didn't have a lot myself," Jennifer said, "but I'm a firm believer that if each person does what they are able we can change the world. As I got into my car that day, I saw a man sitting on the ground who had taken a bag from me. I watched him take the sandwich out and read the note taped to it as a huge smile enveloped his face. I'll never forget that moment."

Within six months Jennifer founded Brunch Club, a nonprofit that expands her initial effort. The group has provided food, essential hygiene items, socks, blankets and words of encouragement to thousands of people experiencing homelessness in San Diego.

"The conversations that have happened, the tears and the community togetherness have been unbelievable," Jennifer said. "It's beautiful. I'm now working on putting health and wellness programs in place to help people transition out of homelessness and into jobs.[4]

Your real self goes against the status quo. It's a radical act to be truly you. It threatens every dogma, groupthink and tradition our culture holds in high regard. You tapping into your most authentic self sets you apart as an individual. And the result of that change is huge.

Say you commit yourself to growing all your own salad greens for an entire year. See if you can calculate the amount of dollars you will cumulatively save and pounds of food you will produce. The fuel that won't be combusted transporting salad greens across the country, state or county. The packaging that won't be used.

Or, maybe you decide to review what you throw out in the trash each week or month and commit to reducing it by 80%. As a family or individual, you'll consider packaging when you buy things. You'll separate recyclables. You'll compost paper, cardboard, food scraps and yard waste like grass clippings and leaves. You'll employ reusable shopping bags at the checkout line. You'll make coffee at home and pour it into reusable travel mugs. You'll buy ingredients instead of prepared, processed, overly packaged food. You'll make a game with your household to see how little you can actually throw away.

If you're depressed and sluggish, it affects all of you from your cells to your imagination. In order to change your life, you're going to have to start by increasing your energy. It won't happen overnight — but it will happen if you relearn how to play. Yes, play! Run around with a young child. Join a pickup soccer league. Go wander around in the woods or start taking a quick walk around the block after dinner. Draw while you watch TV. Better yet, spend one night (or seven) a week without turning the TV on at all. Suddenly, there is a whole lot more time. Take a different route to work. Put a small raised bed in your backyard for essential cooking ingredients like herbs or garlic; hang small planters for herbs on kitchen walls; establish a small aquaponics setup over your family's fish tank. Once a week, go somewhere or do something you've never done before. Do a cartwheel. Hang upside down.

I've always believed theoretically in the power of reinvention: a theory that none of us is ever so trapped we can't stand up and make our lives anew. If you've got itchy feet, a loss of hope or are just fed up with the humdrum hootchie-koo of daily life, get a copy of *Finnegans Wake* and a bus ticket and call me in the morning. Because how you deal with the issue *is* the issue. Because there are so many easy, common-sense ways to stop our suffering on a personal, environmental and macro level. All you have to do is shift your thinking about what's normal and what or who you should be. It's time to stop existing and start L-I-V-I-N'.

The founding principles of Buddhism are the Four Noble Truths: the truth of suffering (*dukkha*), the truth of the cause of suffering, the truth of the end of suffering and the truth of the path that leads us from suffering (*magga*). So life is suffering. Need we be reminded? Suffering is universal while also being unique to each of us. But *dukkha* also refers to the temporary which includes all our joys. Nothing is permanent. The second truth deals with what causes suffering: desire and attachments. We fill our lives up seeking something outside of ourselves to make us happy, instead of feeling the calm that can come in each moment of being centered. We want life to be something it isn't, or we want to be people we are not. We chase unattainable things and inevitably feel disappointed when people don't do as we want or things don't work out as we wish. There is freedom from all of this: the third truth. Letting go of the past or some invented future and instead living in the present moment liberates us. Freedom saves us from the disappointment of a partner, boss, job or anyone else not doing what we want. The end of suffering comes from this detached, empathic space.

Shaking things up is not that hard to learn. And the residual effects will change you so dramatically for the better and make your life so much happier, it seems silly not to at least have a go at a few things that can simultaneously simplify your life, lessen your carbon footprint and inject your human experience with regular doses of fun, interest, health and creativity.

If you don't put up with it, it won't happen. If you refuse to be bested by a physical ailment, you won't be. If you won't stay in a relationship with an abusive partner, he or she will no longer be able to abuse you. If you don't allow a company you buy from to use unethical business practices, you'll put your money where companies give back. If you won't put food in your body that's been treated with chemicals or raised inhumanely, then you will only put good things in.

Bart, an old-timer who lives around the corner from Better Farm, always tells me not to give up. "If you think you can't do it," he says, "you've got to."

We've all got our routines. We get up around the same time every day, have some version of how we get ready for work or play; we often use the same routes to and from our destinations. We eat certain foods. We call certain people. We shop at certain stores. For many of us, these routines feel safe. But they don't always feel particularly eventful or fulfilling. We're bored to death.

Sometimes, we act out. Often we seek something adventurous or mind-numbing in order to slog through the perceived banality of daily life. Boredom breeds all sorts of negative behaviors: extramarital affairs, gambling, drug use, compulsive spending and alcoholism all come to mind. But there are other ways to break up the monotony of our lives in positive ways. So what holds us back from having a new perspective?

What does the world lose by you not being your realest, most honest, open self? What is the risk you run by not going after your deepest motivations and loves? The truth is, the universe needs you more than your unfulfilling job needs you. Humanity needs you more than the partner you feel weighed down by. We have to stop being lulled to sleep by the status quo.

Josey Baker, owner of the successful Josey Baker Bread company and cofounder at The Mill bakery and coffee shop in San Francisco, decided to change when his daily life turned boring. After graduating college in 2005, Josey moved to San Francisco with some friends in the hopes of landing what he saw as a dream job at UC Berkeley developing science curriculum. "Lo and behold my dreams came true," he said, "and I spent five years at the Lawrence Hall of Science writing teacher's guides and children's books."

But what began with vigor turned lackluster. By Josey's fourth anniversary there, the thrill was gone so he promised himself he'd leave by the end of his fifth year. In the meantime, Josey took classes and volunteered doing therapeutic work. He planned to go back to school for psychology and eventually become a therapist.

"When I missed all the deadlines for applying to school the following fall," he said, "it hit me clear as day: it all felt like a chore. The truth was that I didn't know what I wanted to do next; I was just trying to do something. But missing those deadlines sent me back to the drawing board. Then my good buddy George came through town with a sourdough starter and suggested that I try baking a loaf. I'd never baked bread before and didn't even know that one could bake good bread at home. But George gave me some friendly instructions, left me with a little lump of that magical stuff, and a few days later I baked my first loaf."

That bread had Josey hook, line and sinker. "From that point on the mission was obvious: bake as often as I can. Soon enough I had too many loaves to eat, too many to store in my freezer, too many to give away, so I started selling them. A few months later I quit my job — I'd started tending bar to get by — and started baking full-time." Within a year Josey had a book deal and was working on opening his own bakery. And to stay connected to the community in which he works, Josey sources as many local ingredients as possible, even bringing in wheat from less than 100 miles away.[5]

We have to be ready to recognize synchronicity! What if Josey had never baked that loaf of bread? Because he was willing to try something new, he was open to change. Such opportunities are put before us every day; we just fail to see them.

It is courageous to be vulnerable. It is strong to be spiritual and open. It is wise to respond with love. But it's not how most people live. So as you open up, smile more, feel more relaxed, do more for the environment and live more independently, you're going to freak some people out. You will feel pressured to shut back down. You will spend some of your time worrying and being afraid. You will wonder what people think of you. But just as you have been afraid of change before now, so too are the people around you. That's okay: their curiosity means you're doing something inspiring. Try to take it as a compliment.

Welcome the questions. Embrace the confusion.

Think of all the excuses you have for not changing your life. Is organic food too expensive? Do you not have enough time to sew, work on that painting, practice the piano or tend the garden? Are you financially dependent on someone who's pulling the strings?

Start small. Spend just five minutes in the morning looking out the window at a bird feeder. Make time once a week for yoga. Use part of your lunch break at work to walk around the block or sit under a tree. Turn off your TV. *Make the loaf of bread.* Try to pay attention to how much time every day, in minutes, you spend worrying. Force yourself to replace that exact amount of minutes doing something fun, creative or productive.

Take all your excuses, ball them up and throw them atop the floating island of plastic in the middle of the Pacific Ocean. Organic produce has more nutritional content than generic. You're actually getting a whole lot more for your money. And if you have the cash for beer, fast food, a hair cut, cigarettes, cable TV or convenience-store coffee, you also have the cash to upgrade your eating habits to organic and local. Buying ingredients over processed meal items is cheaper in the grand scheme of things. Organic seeds — which will give you a bounty of delicious food — are a fraction of the cost of generic produce by the pound at your local supermarket. Buying ingredients and seeds instead of processed, prefab food will save you a ton of cash, reduce your health care costs and give you more energy.

Ask more questions. Don't look at How Things Are and throw up your hands. Ask yourself why there seem to be more intense floods, hurricanes and snowstorms with increasing regularity. Question why cancer rates are so high. Think about what you are contributing to and taking out of the world. Investigate your boredom. Find the cure.

Empower the naysayers to be more positive by educating them. Invite them over for a farm-to-table dinner party. Have them join you on your next adventure. Host a Top Chef competition featuring a vegetable your garden grew in abundance.

Much of the negativity directed toward you when you make loving, environmentally conscious changes in your life may be born of others' befuddled insecurity. There are people in this world whose disconnect runs so deep that they are automatically threatened by people who live unafraid, curious, open lives. Courageous people invoke terror in people who are weaker. Anger, judgment, gossip, doubt and criticism: these can all be behaviors of a person unwilling to examine his or her own life. Such messaging offers an opportunity for you to let all that crap go.

Dealing with this harsh side effect of making changes is hard work. Being deliberate about what you eat, how you act and how you spend your time arouses suspicion and will draw undue amounts of attention to you. You will at times feel like what you are doing is in vain. You will doubt yourself. And then you will hopefully get brave again and keep on going.

Four out of ten Americans say they are without a satisfying sense of purpose in their lives. And research has shown that having a sense of purpose improves wellness, reduces the odds of becoming depressed and may even extend life expectancy.[6]

This is a process. You're not going to wake up tomorrow and have all the answers. But you can decide today to do something new. You can't change everything all at once — but you can change something right now. The ongoing actions, however small, of you doing better things and spending better time have very large results.

Chapter 9

Community

T HE MOST CENTRAL FOCUS of our sense of belonging and safety lies in our sense of community. We seek to feel connected — whether it's to our families, our lovers or our neighbors. And the nucleus of any community is the home — which, for many of us, is the greatest exhibit of our status and success.

Research shows that people need a few basic things in order to feel fulfilled and happy. We need work that brings us a sense of purpose, joyful experiences, a sense of autonomy and feelings of connectedness to each other, our families and homes.[1]

Volunteers from Better Farm, Redwood Neighborhood Association and Hearts for Youth in 2013 host a seed-planting workshop for children at Redwood's Community Greenhouse.
CREDIT: HEATH PHOTOGRAPHY

Local volunteers get together for an Earth Day cleanup in downtown Redwood, 2013. Credit: Nicole Caldwell

Yet we repeatedly isolate ourselves, experiencing a sense of aloneness even in big cities where we are surrounded by millions of people. Too many of us feel dissatisfied, limited and purposeless. Much of this comes from our modern ways of living. We bust our humps just to make rent, we exist entirely separate from nature and we spend our free time doing passive activities like watching television or surfing the Internet. We lack the basic skills to provide for ourselves, and we neglect our imaginations by not engaging in creative endeavors. Without survival skills, without the experience of cultivating our own food and without regularly flexing our creative muscles, we have grown dependent on capitalism, the workforce and decisions made by politicians who are even more detached from our lives than we are. For goodness sake: we're the only living things actually paying cash to live on the planet.

What we call community is made of the people living in any common place, or a group sharing the same interests, religion or disposition.

But community is also a multigenerational process by which towns are created and nurtured by decades of family businesses, years of hardships and successes and the people who come to live and die within their towns' boundaries. Community suggests a group of people who over time grow into one another and learn to function as a unit. We might think of community as a gesture of inclusiveness and acceptance. It's camaraderie. Whether this banding together is born of discrimination, a shared sense of purpose or a common set of responsibilities, community is what anchors us in our civilizations.

Ubuntu, or human kindness, is a Bantu term from South Africa referring specifically to our humanness. The word invokes a sense of connectedness among all living things and fosters a sense of community: I am who I am because of who we all are. The philosophy of *Uubuntu* is in step with the changes needed to secure an economically and environmentally sustainable future.

Ubuntu is practiced when we see the people we interact with and the world we live in as mirrors. We create each other, we are influenced by each other; what we do to each other and the Earth we do to ourselves. *Ubuntu* dictates true openness to everyone, from strangers to our closest allies. *Ubuntu* acknowledges our uniqueness. People who adhere to *Ubuntu* are in this together. They enable their communities to be better.

The North Country where Better Farm is situated is a strange and beautiful place — and the Redwood community in particular is a perfect case study in community and the practice of *Ubuntu.* Nowhere before have I seen so much familiarity among neighbors, so many helping hands or such a vibrant barter system in place. Before 2009, my dwellings were oases from the world outside. Suburban homes and neighborhoods are often isolated fortresses by design. City living has such a high turnover rate, it's a real challenge to know your neighbors or even the person living in the apartment next door.

When you lift the lid of a community like Redwood and begin to learn about the mechanisms that make it turn, you uncover a world of personalities, quirks and details you'd never guess existed. A strong community provides support for the young and old as well as anyone

betterArts hosts an open mic poetry reading at Better Farm for the public, 2013.
CREDIT: NICOLE CALDWELL

in need. But community also gives those in it a sense of belonging and pride. People feel like they are part of something larger than themselves. Community therefore becomes a cure for the isolation so many of us suffer from.

Community is healing in a lot of ways — not the least of which is neurological. When we have in-person exchanges, we release oxytocin and neurotransmitters that naturally reduce stress and induce trust. A 20-second hug releases enough oxytocin to lower our blood pressure, reduce the physical effects of stress, fight fatigue and infections and lower our heart rates.[2]

Better Farm's surrounding Redwood community is a solar system of humanity. Military veterans live alongside fishers who've never left New York State who live alongside liberals, artists and roofers. Toyota trucks with plastic Buddha sculptures duct-taped to the dashes roll by watering holes in which two-dollar Genny Lights are sipped by wiry old men while they debate NASCAR, the finer points of capital punishment and gun control. Not everyone likes each other — but just about everyone does something to benefit the community in some way.

People from Better Farm and betterArts help local volunteers add a fresh coat of
paint to a building in downtown Redwood in 2011. From left are Sarah Hawkins,
Natasha Frangadilla Pietila, Elizabeth Musoke and Jessie Vogel.
Credit: Nicole Caldwell

A person gets cancer, a fundraiser spaghetti dinner is planned. The post office's paint peels, and a community group scrapes and repaints it. Every day around here, people are stopping in at each other's homes to make sure they have enough to eat, have enough fuel or wood or propane, are in need of nothing. People help each other farm. Split each other's wood. Community members gather together, solicit donations and secure a location to host a completely free Thanksgiving dinner with all the fixings for anyone who would like to participate.

No matter how much the cast and crew of Better Farm goes out in the community to volunteer or lend a hand, the community always seems to be here in greater amounts helping. No matter how any of us tries to repay the favors and gifts bestowed upon us, more arrives. In Redwood you're judged not by the dollar amount on your pay stubs, but by how much you contribute to the community in which you live.

This is how neighborhood barter systems and close-knit groups thrive.

For example: It's October, and a load of logs is dropped off at Better Farm by a man who has been cutting trees on some property a few miles away. The wood needs to be sectioned, split and stacked. It's likely to take a few hours each or every other day for at least a week or two. I run into Glenn, my next-door neighbor, the same afternoon. "I see you've got some wood down at your place," he says, and points at me. "Floydy and I'll be down in the morning to get 'er started. How's ten?"

I go out to Butterfield Lake on a sub-zero day in February to continue demolition work on a little cottage I'm rebuilding. Doc, a neighbor and good friend from down the road, is already out there. The 70-year-old is standing on the roof taking a reciprocating saw to the beams. "Where you guys been?" he shouts, and laughs. "I got out here three hours ago!"

betterArts raises the funds to construct a pavilion next to the Art Barn. Doc, Mollica, Scott, Allen, Carl and anyone else who stops in throughout the day dig postholes to pour footers for the four-by-fours, cross brace the structure and throw on a metal roof.

Darwin "Doc" Whitcomb helps to construct a pavilion next to the Art Barn at Better Farm. Credit: Kathryn Mollica

Scott drops off brush from clients' lawns next to the bonfire pit for the people at the farm to use on Friday nights. Matt drops in after his shift at the hospital to help set up for a music festival. Eileen comes by to organize the arts 'n' crafts in the Art Barn. Carl spends entire days helping me put in a new shower stall or create a stone backsplash for a new pellet stove.

Of course, not all places are like this.

Ferdinand Tönnies in his 1887 book *Gemeinschaft und Gesellschaft* discussed contrasting modes of social organization and community. While most societies will demonstrate traits from multiple models of community, Tönnies simplified the distinctions in order to demonstrate two basic ways in which we create our social worlds. *Gemeinschaft* (a communal society) has several identifying factors: shared perspectives, in-person social interaction, common views on societal norms, a sense of natural will and behavior monitored by non-governmental entities such as families and religious or peer groups. You see this sort of community design in rural, older neighborhoods where families have been established for long periods of time. *Gesellshaft* (associational society) describes more modern societies where groups demonstrate superficial relationships, self-interested motives and status-quo solidarity maintained by a formal authority such as government.[3] The push of industrialized culture leading into World War II left many people feeling isolated. The flooding of suburbs in the US following that conflict is a model of people fleeing what they perceived as a suffocating sense of *Gesellshaft* in search of a more personalized model of *Gemeinshaft*. But what they found was quite different.

The design of those post-war suburbs is still utilized today — even though at their basic structure, they neglect to deliver public centers conducive to enhancing community. We ran from impersonal, urban centers directly into suburbs unwittingly designed with the same superficiality we were so desperate to escape. Strip malls scattered about town prevent people from visiting a specific common area to socialize and reduce walking traffic; they limit community atmosphere and cause an inconsistent rate of interactions between residents. What we missed when we designed towns was the obvious community sensibility formed by authentic contact with one another. Instead, we tried to manufacture interrelationship with neighborhood master plans and gated communities. But we forgot what actually connects people to their neighbors: the land base and each other. You can't fake a community with clever marketing schemes and cookie-cutter houses without a true town center. You can't wear nametags and expect everyone to become characters from "Leave It to Beaver."

Neighborhood and town communities have been on the demise ever since the US became a drive-in culture. Taking the place of actual communities, we now have a false friendliness that businesses put out as a means of manipulating the public's nostalgia for community atmosphere. Telemarketers have to follow close scripts that include robotic, friendly-sounding greetings. Credit card companies send out promotional offers that refer to potential customers by their first name, inviting them into a so-called community of card-carriers.

A *sense of community* has become one of the largest selling points for new subdivisions and towns across the US. Developers boast of this and refer prospective buyers to community-building centers, promoters and boards. Real estate centers rip off true communities by making ads for houses that blatantly suggest choosing the right house will ensure entrance into a strong community. The popularity of these claims proves that that there are millions of people on the move, seeking out true community.

And lack of true community leads to empty-shell interactions. Television is a tool people use to replace thoughtful discourse while at home with their loved ones or friends. TV shows replace the weather as the topic for small talk with strangers. Without a coherent sense of community within a town or neighborhood, family life disintegrates; families on their own cannot possibly take on all the responsibilities a community of many can provide. Married couples cannot exist in a vacuum, and marriages implode. Children are alienated without diverse, frequent interactions.

Might there be a way to create a sense of community without it being corporatized and homogenized?

On a micro scale, some people live communally: you take your community and put it under one roof. Communal homes are hubs for

Sustainability student Elyna Grapstein (left), betterArts resident Kevin Carr (middle) and Better Farm volunteer Matt Smith (at right) teach children how to make their own instruments during a blues festival in Alexandria Bay, New York.
CREDIT: NICOLE CALDWELL

neighborhood potlucks, gardening, creative shares like music and other good stuff. The key to collectives like this are people with a shared commitment to enhancing the group, contributing individually to a larger project and learning how to let go of the small annoyances that pop up for any group trying to work together. The inevitable lack of privacy forces you to keep yourself honest. You're held to a higher standard because there is nowhere to hide.

Communal living can transform assisted living situations for the elderly, disabled or orphaned into wonderful opportunities. Senior centers such as Camelot Cohousing in Massachusetts and Fellowship Community in New York offer the aging an alternative to nursing homes. Each cooperative has different offerings: art studios and shops on the property, shared chores and responsibilities, family-style dining or several small private houses facing out into a central courtyard.

At Wood Green, a collection of bungalows for senior citizens in Britain, a flock of chickens are kept to help residents fight loneliness and feelings of isolation. Seniors hatch, raise and care for the birds. There are also hen-based activities — art, dance and songs — inspired by poultry. The results of that program were so successful that eight pilot sites have since been developed copying the design. Residents involved in the program reported feeling a sense of purpose since having the birds around.

In the US, more than a dozen Bay Area mansions are being occupied as communal living spaces, according to a *San Francisco Chronicle* report. The trend — there are more than 50 co-living arrangements throughout the city — is in part a response to the economy. San Francisco rent has recently soared to the highest in the United States. Communal living fractionates that number while providing a sense of connection through shared garden plots, family-style dinners and common areas for music, art or socializing. Living like this also promotes sustainability — from growing food on-site to using less energy.[4]

Cohousing, an architectural concept that commonly utilizes 20 to 30 private condos with shared areas such as community centers and gardens, is an increasingly popular way to enjoy a tight-knit community, private housing and shared culture. Common threads among cohousing communities are shared meals several times a week, community events, shared responsibilities and decisions made by consensus. There are well over 200 cohousing neighborhoods listed in a directory published by the Cohousing Association of the United States. Roughly that many are also under development.[5]

In his book *An Agricultural Testament*, father to the organic food and compost movements Sir Albert Howard discussed what he called Diamond City designs. The concept, originating with one Dr. George Vivian Poore and expanded by Dr. L. J. Picton in a 1924 piece in *The British Medical Journal*, pairs communal living with land stewardship. Diamond cities would be 25 homes set in a diamond shape on four acres, with all living rooms facing south. In the center would be a shared garden looked over by one full-time person (and helpers as necessary), who among his jobs would empty bathroom waste every day into the gardens as manure. Food scraps would go to chickens and the compost pile. The idea, though never widely adopted, would certainly change the face of how we design neighborhoods in our cities, suburbs and the countryside.[6]

During summer programming at Better Farm, we've had up to 14 people staying here for a month at a time. This living situation allows for all kinds of annoyances: sometimes people don't clean up after themselves or neglect to carry their fair share of responsibility. But the benefits are enormous. The pride that goes along with constructing something as a group that will be around long after people disband and return to their daily lives fosters a sense of history. Walking the grounds on farm tours, we point things out like the greenhouse assembled out of discarded windows by Craig, Jody, Brian, Chris, Clayton and several others. Or the birdhouse cabin, erected during a memorial celebration.

Better Farm Dinner Party, 2014.
CREDIT:
BETTER FARM ARCHIVES

Then there's the *Be Here Now* benefit of working together. My favorite of these experiences is preparing meals with people in the big farmhouse kitchen, or — even better — sitting down to a meal at the 12-foot table complete with two church pews. There is nothing like sharing a meal and conversation at a table with several North Country natives, a father and son from Scotland, an Israeli couple, a group of French women road-tripping through Canada and New York, students staying for the summer and artists-in-residence. The table is a true melting pot. And because we're all here for a common purpose, we are afforded an ideas exchange that is second to none in its inspiring nature.

Conversations, in fact, are at the heart of any functioning community. The arts of conversation and storytelling are binding agents for humanity. And yet they can be the first attributes we lose when we opt for texting or email over face-to-face.

The strong social ties in a community are what psychologist Susan Pinker calls the *village effect.* Her book by the same title explored the social contacts we all need as humans in order to thrive. These points of contact can be a public area downtown where people pass each other regularly to get to places like the post office or bank. Steve Jobs mimicked this central square in an office building design for a new Pixar headquarters. The atrium was in the center of everything, with all hallways, bathrooms and offices opening up to it. People had to walk by each other to get anywhere. This design forced interaction and encouraged conversation among people with different traits and skillsets. For Jobs, these regular encounters translated to daily opportunities for growth.[7]

At Better Farm, the kitchen and gardens are our atrium. Artists-in-residence are required to contribute several hours a week to farm work; many opt to be out in the garden with our sustainability students. The conversation, education and enjoyment out there as these perfect strangers mutually get their hands dirty are staggering. Back inside, overnight guests prepare meals alongside long-term lodgers, students, teachers and artists. It's a level playing field, where an 18-year-old college student can sit alongside a 50-something, professional painter and each can learn from the other.

But in the so-called real world, we've made isolation chambers instead of village effects. In my apartments throughout Manhattan and Brooklyn, there was only one neighbor I ever got to know. Marge was in her 80s and would scuttle over to knock on my door if a great program was on PBS or she needed help reaching one of her pots or pans. We'd exchange niceties, and I'd be back in my shoebox studio, on the phone or working on my computer. Why do we choose to live this way?

Being separated from each other emotionally, intellectually or physically reduces our abilities to empathize and breeds narcissism. And it's not just us; we're now doing a disservice to future generations by raising them to see overdependence on technology as normal. Classrooms are virtual, friendships are virtual and children are outside less and less.

Point of fact: Children between the ages of 8 and 18 spend, on average, 7.5 hours a day plugged in to their electronic devices, according to a Kaiser Family Foundation Study. And there are more young children who know how to use an iPad, get online or play a video game than can swim or ride a bike. Yet study after study shows that kids who play around in nature are consistently more creative, healthier, inquisitive and even demonstrate a higher rate of joy.[8] What are we doing to our children?

With the overwhelming nature of the cyberworld, where online profiles can create virtual personalities, we are ever-connected while simultaneously ever-disconnected. We've as a culture accepted an illusion of connection — text messages, trolling social media, online dating and video games played against people worldwide — while in reality we are ever more separated. The anonymity of the online world forces each of us into our own, individual heads. Without the constant ricochet of ideas close-knit groups afford, we are prone to depression, anxiety, doubt and surrendering to our deepest fears and misconceptions.

Isolation prevents an individual from tempering his or her thoughts and expression; it subjects a person to succumbing to anxiety and fear. Being lonely also breeds contempt and resentment. That in turn can cause acting out — whether in relationships, at home or with society.

Anyone who has ever been in a bad relationship or suffered from depression will tell you how confusing it is to be isolated with the manipulation of another person or one's own mind, without friends or family to offer insight or alternative opinions. Being alone all the time prevents accountability. And that's something you can't really gain in a chat room or on a social media site.

In the US we see more school shootings. Random violence. People go so inward and get so sick without a shared sense of responsibility for each other or the accountability a healthy community provides. We see unbelievably high rates of prisoners returning to a penal system that doesn't rehabilitate. We see unhealthy relationships get worse.

We can stop all these cycles by building community and becoming closer with the natural environment. Because when we connect to the world, we connect better to all living beings — including each other. Nature is our common ground.

Connectivity dissolves our self-obsessions. One of the most trusted methods for helping individuals suffering from addiction overcome their substance- or behavior-based reliance is to encourage them to connect with something larger than themselves.

Alcoholics Anonymous utilizes a *higher power* approach. If a person believes there is a god, universal being or transcendental consciousness, then he or she is less likely to opt for the depressive nature of alcohol dependence. Be that higher power nature, god, family or community, reality shows us that the less anonymous we are and the more we connect with that power, the more empathic, calm, nurturing and thoughtful we become.

The return rate for state prisoners in the US is staggering. Within three years of their release, 67.8% of former prisoners end up back in jail, according to Bureau of Justice Statistics. That same source found 76.6 % of all former inmates return to jail within five years. To combat these numbers, some prisons across the country have begun to utilize a new approach to rehabilitation: gardening. The goals of such programs are to train inmates in landscaping skills for future job prospects, and as rehabilitation because gardening causes people to reconnect with their feelings, community, nature and themselves.

Prisoners enrolled in these programs are now part of a new statistic. San Quentin's program, called Planting Justice, reports a recidivism rate of just 10% for those who go through the gardening program. In Connecticut, each of the state's 18 prisons has a garden program. As of 2015, not one inmate graduating from the program has returned to jail. In addition, the Connecticut programs in one year put around 35,000 pounds of produce into prison kitchens. That single feat saved taxpayers $20,000.[9]

The reason for these correlations is pretty simple: being in nature has been proven to lower sensations of anger, fear and stress — all things prisoners live with in excess. Research conducted at hospitals and businesses found that even a single plant in a room has reductive effects on anxiety. And working together toward a common good promotes empathy and compassion.

So if we could encourage people to connect to nature — and do it in a way that benefits the community and fosters a sense of responsibility — we'd be covering a lot of ground that would boost our levels of happiness, empathy, sense of belonging, health and our ability to heal the planet.

Researchers in Australia, Canada, Sweden and the United States found that children in natural environments with grass or wooded areas participated in higher levels of fantasy play rooted in creativity, imagination and language. Children in manufactured play structures involved themselves in more competition-based play to establish social hierarchies.[10]

The 2014 US Farm Bill was the first of its kind to acknowledge veterans as a brave new class of beginning farmers and ranchers. This recognition means vets are eligible for additional government assistance for agricultural programs such as lower interest rates on farm-related loans. But more interesting is the potential of farming to help heal psychological effects of war and help individuals rejoin civilian life. This farm bill is a nod to the healing effects of digging in the dirt.

You make community by making community work fun. You motivate people by giving them something exciting to do and giving them a sense of ownership over their work and lives. You build community by engaging people and making them accountable.

*Better Farm
volunteers pitch
in to help move
Redwood's
community
greenhouse in 2014.
From left are Allison
Bachner, Kathryn
Mollica and Xuan
Du.*
CREDIT: NICOLE CALDWELL

Maybe you don't live in a place conducive to the village effect. So what? You can make your own. Anyone can go out and get to know his or her neighbors. Walk up to your coworker's desk and start talking. Call your friends and ask them out to coffee. If they live across the country, save your dollars and plan a trip. Call instead of texting. On the next nice day wander around the block, look people in the eyes and smile when you walk by. Establish a community garden or compost pile.

Use technology to complement interactions instead of replacing them. Make a social media group to get the word out about fun community activities. Use the barter system as currency. Form an email list of volunteers for upcoming projects. Start a blog where members of the community can contribute. Start acting like the people you live with are on your team and plan projects accordingly. Do things together. Have a sit-down, home-cooked meal on a regular basis with the people in your house. Ask people real questions about their day. Give more compliments and say thank you.

There are so many things to do! Community newsletters. Neighborhood cleanups. Tool sharing. Block parties. Potlucks. Book clubs. Tree plantings. Gallery openings. Festivals. Barn raisings. Cohousing.

You can create a village effect on a global scale, too. Even without leaving your home. Even without spending a ton of money.

Iowan Lillian Weber sews one dress a day to send to Africa for children in need. She began the project in 2011 when she was 96 in support of the nonprofit organization Little Dresses for Africa. The nonprofit's goal is to send a message to little girls that they are worthy.

The Kindness Team is an organization whose sole purpose is to infiltrate the world with the transformative power of kindness. Specifically focused on utilizing kindness to help end hunger in America, the group invites individuals to film themselves discussing their ideas about what it means to be kind. Personal stories are shared in an online video format. This network builds a community based on this central idea.[11]

Moving to the North Country forced me to slow down. Forced me to accept the drop-by, unexpected visitor. Retaught me the art of storytelling. Of running into people and having a 20-minute conversation when all you're trying to do is mail a letter at the post office. Of not checking the clock every two minutes and instead making time for people. Of allowing unexpected occurrences to change the to-do list for a day.

That doesn't mean communal living is easy or always pleasant. In a living situation like Better Farm, which is a business and a living space, the community changes almost daily during our busiest months. It's more of a temporary training ground than a permanent living situation. That can be difficult to get used to: just when you grow accustomed to one family dynamic, people leave and others arrive. In this state of constant flux, it can be a challenge to learn how to ask for privacy and to demand alone time. But these concessions — actually character-builders — are so far outweighed by the positives. It seems almost silly to think we'd stay separate intentionally when the benefits of cohousing, communal living, community gardens and barter systems are so bountiful.

Experience after experience teaches us at Better Farm that living together, neighborhood events, shared responsibilities and community outreach consistently enrich our lives.

We build community at the farm by offering year-round events that invite locals to visit the campus and interact with an international pool of students and artists staying here. Farm tours, festivals, gallery

Kathryn Mollica leads a farm tour, 2013.

CREDIT: BETTER FARM ARCHIVES

openings, volunteer days, workshops, movie nights and harvest dinners all encourage interaction, conversation, ideas and creativity.

Community building helps the environment. Cooking dinner in one kitchen with a group of people utilizes less energy than ten people cooking in ten different kitchens. It utilizes less waste, as buying in bulk or growing your own requires less packaging, if any at all. Staying in a house with other people sharing utilities requires less energy consumption. In the US, we live in ways where our homes contribute more to environmental degradation than cars. Communal living changes that statistic.

In our towers of isolation, it's every man for himself. We compete endlessly. And we're killing ourselves, each other and the planet in the process. Wars. Huge, mindless corporations. GMOs. Unethical business practices. School shootings. Record diagnoses of ADD. Overmedicated children. Stepford wives. We have forgotten how much we need each other. We've become so fixated on our privacy, we've forgotten about our humanity. If we could just cooperate and work toward the common good we all desire, we could change our culture from one of isolation to one of inclusion. We can create community in our lives, from the workplace to our homes and everywhere in between. Investing in our communities with our time and hearts gives huge returns on our levels of happiness, health, sense of purpose and empathy. When we can pair that community effort with responsible stewardship of the Earth and creative undertakings, those returns multiply exponentially.

Chapter 10

It's Hip to Be Green

IT IS HIP TO BE GREEN. It's cool to give a damn about the world itself and all the humans, animals, crustaceans, invertebrates and plants who call it home. It is sweet to be motivated by love. It is fair to work peacefully toward our goals for this and future generations. It is smart

Yes we can!
Better Farm's version of
Rosie the Riveter, 2014.
Credit: Better Farm Archives

to consider the planet before choosing how we live, vote, shop, eat and survive.

The green movement has historically been allocated to liberal hallways of discussion; it's been marginalized politically to seemingly represent the agenda of the few. But good science and updated technology have transformed the discussion from one associated with bleeding-heart liberalism and hippiedom into a much broader conversation about a topic affecting every single living creature on the planet.

A renewed global interest in green living, organic food and self-sufficiency means a renewed opportunity to push for change never before imagined. It's only a matter of time before consumers will be able to look at food packaging and know whether ingredients were genetically modified. More scientific data on issues such as climate change, water runoff and topsoil levels give voters leverage with politicians, and consumers leverage with farmers. People are in a powerful position in which they can ask for certain standards and Big Ag, corporations and politicians would be smart to provide answers and solutions sooner rather than later.

The green movement is growing. Virtually all automakers now have fuel-efficient or hybrid options. More than 250 honeybee hives were registered in New York City in 2013 according to the *New York Times;* and the New York City Beekeepers Association in 2013 boasted 480 members (up from just 25 in 2007). More and more 20- and 30-somethings are ditching cubicle culture in favor of homesteading. During the 2009 recession, people waited out the job market by flooding application pools for ashrams, artist retreats and ecovillages. Petco sells a basic at-home aquaponics kit. Neiman Marcus offers a $100,000 chicken coop.[1]

The green movement has the endorsement of celebrities. Cameron Diaz, Leonardo DiCaprio, Jessica Alba and countless others have jumped on the green bandwagon. There are green alternatives to everything from organic dry cleaners to limited-ingredient dog food.

The Better Theory shows that with the good comes the bad. And so it is that green living brings with it greenwashing: disinformation pushed by an organization to present an environmentally responsible

Better Farm volunteer Devesh Doobay helps to spread hay in the gardens, 2014.
CREDIT: NICOLE CALDWELL

Better Farm volunteer Aaron Youngs fills buckets with newly made dirt from the compost pile, 2013.
CREDIT: NICOLE CALDWELL

public image. It's greenwashing when big oil companies tout green technology they use, when that technology is only a tiny part of their business. The irony of car companies getting in on this green game, so-called carbon-neutral airplane hangars and the massive overuse of the word organic are just a few examples of greenwashing in action. A "Sins of Greenwashing" report in 2010 found that 95% of companies claiming to be green were in fact the opposite.[2] So it's fair to say that it takes more than celebrity, more than product placement and more than buying a shampoo with natural herbal extracts to truly live green.

US environmentalism has embarrassingly become about consumerism: *buying green*. We wrap ourselves in fair-trade yoga pants and phthalate-free children's toys and try to use this green labeling to feel better about a consumptive lifestyle.

But truly *living green* requires a shift in how we live our lives. It requires us to take our environment into account first. This is not about buying stuff tagged with an eco-friendly label, or patting yourself on the back for buying a shampoo infused with pure fruit extracts amidst a dizzying list of unpronounceable ingredients. It's not about buying bottled water packaged in individual, recycled plastic containers. It actually has to do with consuming less and giving more.

Thankfully, that too is on the rise.

The prevalence of community gardens in urban neighborhoods demonstrates a renewed interest in buying local, growing your own and working with neighbors toward a common good. And that makes places like Better Farm valuable as hotbeds for training and general education in how to have your own homestead in any setting.

Even rainwater catchment is now widely used as an essential part of truly Better homes and gardens. All previous bans on rainwater catchment in the US have been traded for regulations.

Rainwater catchment was once seen as a threat to local water tables and treatment facilities, which rely on rainwater runoff to fill tanks for processing. But a 2007 study by the Colorado Water Conservation Board and Douglas County found that only 3% of Colorado rain actually reaches a stream or the water table — rendering rainwater catchment inconsequential to public water supply. Legislators in 2009

Local volunteer Bob Laisdell, center, teaches a workshop in 2014 at Better Farm about building with recycled materials. This sauna was created entirely with discarded, used building materials. CREDIT: NICOLE CALDWELL

Nicole Caldwell (left) and Holly Boname enjoy a see saw made from reclaimed materials, 2013. CREDIT: DAVE CIOLLI

revised state code to allow residential homeowners with wells to utilize rainwater and another that allowed for "pilot development projects."[3]

The design of Better Farm allows people to arrive, acquire knowledge, experience and reconnect with their creative tendencies, then to go home and pay it forward. Our purpose here is to equip people with skills necessary to live more self-sufficiently, creatively, lovingly and freely — and to then go out in the world and inspire others to do the same. This work is largely possible because of the revisited interest people are taking in the environment. As ecological problems become more in-your-face and affect more people globally each day, they become impossible to ignore. Better Farm gives people the power to make changes for the better.

And the world is taking notice. The work of individuals, organizations, companies, counties and countries are making the difference all the pessimists said would be impossible.

New Haven Farms is a group of seven gardens in Connecticut established in part on previously vacant lots. The program serves Fair Haven, a part of the city where the majority of residents live below the federal poverty line and seven out of ten are overweight or obese. The organization in 2014 unrolled a free, 20-week wellness program that met three times a week between May and October. Attendees gardened, listened to lectures about health and nutrition and prepared communal meals together.

Extreme deforestation throughout the 20th century along the Brahmaputra River in India led to catastrophic floods and massive erosion. One day in 1979, 16-year-old Jadav Payeng saw snakes that had overheated and died after being washed ashore on a treeless sandbar during a flood. Unable to receive support to plant trees and told nothing could grow along the banks of the Brahmaputra River near which he lived, Jadav Payeng started planting trees on his own. In the ensuing 35 years, Payeng single-handedly created an island forest larger than New York City's Central Park. Molai Forest is now inhabited by tigers, rhinoceroses and elephants.

Kijani Grows is a company in West Oakland, California, that sells aquaponics systems, hosts educational workshops and works with

Sustainability student Jackson Pittman bakes in Better Farm's kitchen, 2013.
CREDIT: NICOLE CALDWELL

Maylisa Jade (left) and Brian Hines-Schwartz harvest veggies at Better Farm in 2012.
CREDIT: NICOLE CALDWELL

teenagers to acquaint them with producing their own food. The company's founder is Eric Maundu, whose inspiration came from his upbringing in Kenya. There, he witnessed the struggles farmers faced growing plants in arid climates that lacked rich soil. Maundu didn't have goals of becoming a farmer. But after earning a degree in electronics and computer science, he learned in 2009 about hydroponics and decided to build his first setup. He has returned to Kenya several times to help establish aquaponics farms there for people to produce their own food.

Another California company, the Los Angeles-based EVO Farm, uses aquaponics to offer the city a new kind of farming model. EVO relies on a network of small, urban farms to provide city dwellers with fresh, locally grown organic food.

In Africa, regreening efforts in southern Niger have meant a food-production spike of 500,000 tons annually. Similar efforts in Ethiopia over the course of a mere 15 years brought villages back from the brink of disappearing and turned desert to forest. Farming communities teamed up to plant trees, cordon off tracts of land from animals and conserve water. These relatively simple methods are now being replicated across one sixth of Ethiopia, with a goal set to have the area fully regreened by 2030.[4]

This is hip. This is possible. And this isn't as hard as you think.

The Future of Farms

We are on a new frontier of food safety. Consumers are learning more about the dangers of all those ingredients on packaged food and changing shopping habits accordingly. But we're also learning more about soil science and becoming aware of what it's going to take to feed Earth's future population.

The UN Commission on Trade and Development in 2014 reported that sweeping changes in agricultural and trade systems are necessary in order to promote biodiversity on farms, reduce fertilizers and additives and create stronger food systems. The report stated, in essence, that small-scale, organic farming is the only way to feed the world.

But what's *small?* The US National Commission on Small Farms puts $250,000 in annual sales as the line in the sand between small- and

Giant Swiss chard harvest at Better Farm, 2013. CREDIT: NICOLE CALDWELL

Sustainability student Elyna Grapstein (left) and betterArts resident Kevin Carr show off a hubbard squash they grew in 2012. CREDIT: NICOLE CALDWELL

large-scale farms. Most cropland in the early 1980s was operated by farms with less than 600 crop acres; today, most cropland is on farms with at least 1,100 acres — and a lot of farms are ten times that size. The reason for the supersizing is simple: bigger farms see bigger profits. But as farm acreage grew, crop and livestock production were separated.[5]

This method for producing crops without livestock has involved an ongoing loss of production fertility. Growing the same thing in the same dirt year after year without the benefit of animals rooting through the land and fertilizing the soil leeches nutrients from the ground. A potato, for example, needs different things from the soil than, say, a broccoli plant.

Conversely, each plant leaves something different behind in the dirt in which it grows. Crops should be getting rotated at least every few years, essentially mimicking the work of nature in forests, prairies and oceans where plants pop up all over in a seemingly random, ever-changing array. Farmers and gardeners are also smart to utilize the help of farm animals to turn over ground, fertilize and for help with composting. But in large-scale agricultural settings, mixed farming like this doesn't happen.

In nature, plants are found with a host of other living organisms. From simple invertebrates to mammals, life cohabits with life. The more living matter, the better. But on mass-produced scales, everything is about the bottom line and the fastest, easiest way to get there. So we dose massive fields of apple trees with pesticides to keep bugs and disease away. We hit plants with fertilizers to artificially boost production. Media campaigns promise it is somehow safe to ingest this stuff. Nothing thrives, save for genetically modified Frankencorn, nutritionally deficient soybeans and apples covered in chemicals you can't wash away.

Give us a break, already!

The future of food rests in the work of small farms and homesteads that adhere to the rhythms of the natural world. We need gardens where cows or pigs can come in to turn over dirt that's then turned over by chickens, where a variety of crops can grow on a rotating basis year after year with only the addition of compost and mulch. Animal waste turns to humus, and everything is used. Top priority is the dirt itself — which retains all the nutrition plants will need.

Having many different kinds of plants means that if one year potatoes do poorly, perhaps turnips and artichokes have excelled. Or if tomatoes suffer a blight, there are peppers and eggplants that are stellar. We are freed from having to depend on perfect conditions for all plants because we have a cornucopia to choose from. Plants enjoy a rotating stock of minerals from massive reserves in the subsoil, unburdened by chemical additives. And if your spinach came out crummy, maybe your neighbor down the street has a boom, and you can swap for those lovely cucumbers you grew.

You see how strong this sort of balance is anytime a forest is destroyed for monocultures. Plants put in the newly cleared soil can grow for a decade without the need for added fertilizers because of deep reserves in the dirt. Before this sort of razing occurs, nature has somehow found a way to promote all forms of life without having to spray chemicals or poisons. Among small populations, disease is contained quickly because there is no mass population of any one thing.

These rules carry over to oceans, rivers, streams, lakes and prairies. Biodiversity allows for a lush life. And this version of growth is one we humans followed Once Upon a Time. We have seen what happens when we disregard the way nature does things.

We've replaced much of our livestock with machines, trading for example horse and plow with tractor and attachments. But the tractor doesn't offer manure and does zero to maintain soil fertility. We cheat nowadays with artificial, chemical-based fertilizers. This began during World War I, when atmospheric nitrogen began being fixed for the manufacture of explosives. We borrowed that science to produce cheap forms of nitrogen, phosphorous and potassium.

After World War II, leftover nitrate munitions were earmarked for agricultural use. These fertilizers do nothing to make the soil actually healthy, however. Growth isn't fed by decay as it is in nature. That means the fertilizer will have to be reapplied year after year in order to produce a strong yield. We essentially zap soil of its strength when we artificially fertilize our ground without giving it the rotting matter (manure, compost) to thrive.

Only a small percentage of nitrogen in artificial fertilizers is actually absorbed by plants. And as the fertilizer kills microbials of the dirt, the remaining added nitrogen is washed away with rainfall through dirt to waterways. Once here, algal blooms are abundant. The algae pulls oxygen from the water, suffocating fish and other aquatic life.

Oceanic dead zones, areas too oxygen-depleted to support life, were found in 49 locations across the world in the 1960s. In 2014, the World Resources Institute listed 479 such locations.[6]

This is not cool. This is not the best we can do.

Studies show that biodiversity even aids us psychologically. Scientists from the University of Sheffield in the United Kingdom found that the more species found in a park, the greater the psychological effects on humans. Our exposure to the Earth encourages closer human-to-human relationships. This connection is found every day, but researchers at the University of Rochester in New York made a concrete connection. Those whose focus was on the human made demonstrated a higher regard for fortune and fame — and this focus contributed to a sense of unease.[7]

You can create a biologically diverse garden easily by mulch gardening. Mulch gardening is a layering method that mimics a forest floor and combines soil improvement, weed removal and long-term mulching in one fell swoop. Also called lasagna gardening or sheet mulching, this process can turn hard-to-love soil rich and healthy by improving nutrient and water retention in the dirt, encouraging favorable soil microbial activity and worms, suppressing weed growth and improving the well-being of plants (all while reducing maintenance!).

All it takes to start mulch gardening is to first lay a barrier such as cardboard down to smother weeds. The cardboard and weeds eventually decompose and turn into compost. On top of the cardboard go dead leaves, grass clippings, compost, several-years-old composted manure and other biodegradables such as old hay. Mulch gardening can range from just a few inches thick to two feet or more, depending on how bad the soil is and how much raw material is available.

These layers cook down and settle quite a bit over time, so layers are constantly being added as they become available; you can even dump food scraps from the kitchen directly into garden rows, bypassing compost tumblers and piles entirely. The cyclical process goes on year-round and works so well that not a single additive or chemical has to be added to the soil.[8]

Ruth Stout is credited with the emergence of the mulch gardening movement. Her iconic 1955 tome *How to Have a Green Thumb Without an Aching Back* was given to me by a friend who picked it up at a stoop sale in Brooklyn the summer I moved to Better Farm. That book, which chronicles Stout's own discovery and methods of mulch gardening, is the reason I first experimented with the practice. I now swear by it.

Think of topsoil as a garden's skin. Manicured, conventional gardens with bare ground between plants scorch the soil's skin and cause sensitivity among plants and soil to temperature, humidity and disease.

When you utilize mulch gardening, you're protecting the soil and plants from all that nonsense. You're using Mother Nature's own blueprint for how to make things grow. All the compostable materials you use in mulch gardening attract earthworms, which absolutely love organic matter. A healthy acre of soil is home to anywhere between one and two million earthworms, each of which is passing its own weight in soil through its body each day.

Vote Earth First

It's fashionable to vote for the environment. And it's high time we started to. In the United States, 2014's midterm elections saw the worst voter turnout since 1942. 1942! You may be really very seriously concerned about economics. Job growth. War chests. Gun control. Abortion. Maybe you are planning on voting for someone you don't like in order to ensure the incumbent gets tossed. Say you're voting based on who's better on women's rights. Gay rights. Civil rights. Health care. Balancing the budget. Supporting our military. Maybe you just really hate Democrats or can't stand Republicans.

Well, listen up. There's one fundamental truth which affects each and every one of us: we live or die based on the condition of the Earth.

CREDIT: NICOLE CALDWELL

*Jackson Pittman (left) and Holly Boname enjoy the beautiful water of Redwood's
Millsite Lake.* CREDIT: NICOLE CALDWELL

We don't get job growth without safe drinking water. There is no debate over gun control without nourishing food. We have no security and no safety without fresh air to breathe. There is one thing that comes before every stance we take in this world and that's the environment. She shields us, clothes us, feeds us, warms us, cools us and only ever operates from a neutral, vibrant place.

It's time to stop carrying on in spite of her and start making moves because of her. These moves come in large part out of where we put our money and whose name we check on our voting ballots. Which politicians are willing to stand up and defend her? Who is unwavering in their devotion to Mother Dearest? Who understands the gravity of our environmental situation and the stakes? Whoever that is, that is whom we need to go out and support. Today. Right now.

Look back in time, several decades. A whole lot of people got together back in those days for an anti-war movement. John Lennon and Yoko Ono staged their bed protests: Hair Peace. Bed Peace. People harnessed their energy and pressured the political arena. And you know what? The US pulled out of Vietnam. It happened. The republic spoke. Why is it so far-fetched to think that, even in this era we might be able to harness that public energy again in order to make big, environmental changes?

Let's abolish fracking once and for all. Let's live to see the end of drilling for oil. Let's establish an overwhelming shift in perspective about how we live our lives in general. If the general public can end wars and push uptight politicians to accept recreational marijuana use, is it so wild to think we could make compost toilets the norm and end our reliance on fracked gas? Or that we could put an end to the endlessly diverted waterways out west? That we could refuse, with the force of millions, to subsidize huge corporations that couldn't care less about us or the Earth?

Do we have to be drowning below sea level or actually run out of wild-caught fish for people to vote for the environment? California shouldn't have to dry out entirely for us to consider our elected officials' stances on water conservation. Glaciers shouldn't have to go the way of the woolly mammoth before we are willing to discuss climate change on a political level. Ditto for lakes and rivers being deemed unfishable, unswimmable before we're willing to vote for someone who will protect our waterways.

Don't wait for every last ounce of oil to be drawn from the ground and every reserve to be cashed in on. Don't let some bigwig frack in every available spot, provide jobs a few years and make some fat cats even fatter before we realize we can't actually eat all those dollar bills.

Give me a break.

> Vote the Environment. She's the only renewable resource on the planet besides hope and love.
>
> Vote Mother Earth. She's the only politician with a literal platform: the ground beneath your feet.
>
> Vote the Planet. Because manufactured meat, farmed salmon and GMOs ain't gonna cut it.

The environment's the most topical news story there is; it's more relevant than any celebrity sound bite or white-collar crime. We're talking climate change. Extinction. Destruction of wild places. Record droughts. Rising sea levels. Severe storms and weather patterns. Dogs and cats, living together! It's all happening while we argue over who we'll vote for based on who gives a crap about health care, birth control or how many bullets can go into a gun. This is like a magician getting you to look at one hand while he sleights with the other.

Stop being so distracted!

It's time to draw the proverbial line in the sand: DO NOT CROSS! We will not let you! This has gone too far. We've had it! Radical acts are in. The status quo is OUT!

It's time to reimagine things. Think big. The end of supermarkets as we know them. The utter refusal on the part of the consumer to buy packaged, processed, poisonous foods. Fossil fuel-free homes and businesses. Schools where children participate in their school lunch program by growing and raising everything consumed in the school cafeteria. Why can't we? Wouldn't that meet horticulture, biology, math and business requirements? Wouldn't that allow our children to be more self-sufficient, less dependent on the hamster wheel their parents are so desperate to get off of?

We should give each other the chance to enjoy the true art of living — of being completely alive, the best versions of our truest selves. Open, untouched spaces. Rainwater catchment systems on every home, shed, barn and greenhouse. More greenhouses. Everywhere. The complete decimation of the gas-powered vehicle, of the septic system, of dammed rivers.

So compost. Cook meals with your friends featuring food fresh from the garden. Love each other and forgive and go love some more. Eat organic. Ditch sugar. Pick up trash, recycle and help to conserve our wild places. And, for goodness sake, be cool and put Mother Dearest first. What good is that voice the world gave you if you don't use it to defend her?

Chapter 11

Start Sustainability Now

RESPONSIBLE STEWARDSHIP of the land and sustainable living are crafts. They are works of art, perhaps of the utmost variety. This art form requires no formal training — in fact, we already innately know how to do it.

Humans are natural leaders, natural innovators and have always been naturally resourceful. But we've misinterpreted our role on the planet. As a culture we've determined that the Earth is here for our use, and we've in turn treated the environment like a commodity. We have an industry for water. For soil.

But our higher level of consciousness allows us to protect. Our ability to take care of each other — not our might — is what sets us apart from other living things. It is our responsibility, not our gift, that distinguishes us. It is time to own up.

There are easy things everyone can do to change their local ecosystem, food habits, communities, health and overall well-being. We don't have to wait around for laws or politicians or policy to change. We are not victims. We are powerful enough to make basic changes at home that will make big ripples. The changes are inexpensive, practical and healthy for everyone. This chapter is a cheat sheet for a whole lot of easy things we can do to green our lives.

Love Your Body

All your work on this planet comes out of you. And the moment you start respecting and loving your own body is the moment you refuse to do anything that would put it in harm's way. Loving your self is the start toward exercise, a healthy whole-food diet and the end of polluting, mindless buying, and disconnection from the real world.

Copy Nature

Mother Nature is one smart lady. From ethics to food production to giving more than you take, look to the land base for lessons on how to live your life. You've got to start trusting the Earth to provide. Everything you need — each and every thing! — exists in the natural world. The planet provides in abundance for your overall wellness, your medicine and your tools. You may have forgotten your faith in this bounty. That doesn't mean it isn't there.

Grow Your Own Food

Growing your own food removes your need for Big Agriculture. By creating your own beds of greens, veggies and even fruit trees, you're taking yourself out of the monster machine that large-scale agriculture has become. There is no reason everyone can't be growing at least some of his or her own food. Even one thing. Even lettuce growing out of reused coffee tins in a sunny kitchen window. If you provide just one vegetable, herb or salad green you love for yourself, you'll be saving exponential amounts of money and fossil fuels otherwise spent in the transportation of that item to you commercially throughout your lifetime. Any fish tank can host an aquaponics array that will give you and your family fresh produce year-round. Herbs can grow in pots hanging from your kitchen walls. Start a community garden with your neighbors if you don't have the time to take care of so much on your own — and then split what you reap.

Ditch the Pesticides

It's a strange notion we've developed, that there ought not be bugs outdoors. This is the stuff of delusions. Yet people somehow make this antithetical notion work in their minds. Have you read the ingredient list on a box or can of pesticide? There is no reason whatsoever to consume food covered in poisonous chemicals. When a pesticide leaches through the soil where it is applied, it ends up inside the food we're growing. It also dives into the water table.

In waterways, pesticides kill millions of fish each year while other aquatic life suffers the consequences of pesticide-contaminated water. Pesticides are known to add to air pollution as a result of pesticide drift, and some play a role in harming the ozone layer. Additionally, pesticides have a resistance to breaking down over time.

Deal with the fact that most bugs in your garden are doing helpful things. The ones that aren't can easily be handled in a way that won't poison you in the process. You will be amazed at the multiple powers marigolds, dish soap, garlic and hot peppers have over pests.

Compost Your Food Scraps

About 20% of what we throw away as waste is actually food. Twenty percent! If no one ever threw a food scrap away ever again that would mean millions of pounds of food scraps each year turning into lush soil for backyard gardeners. Composting would minimize transportation costs associated with hauling garbage away from our homes. And it would nurture the dirt in everyone's backyard.

Whether you feed your food scraps directly to your garden, or to a compost tumbler, or to the earthworms living in a container under your New York City apartment sink, you're creating a sustainable, circular system and limiting what gets added to landfills. If you don't have a garden, take your beautiful black topsoil you create and donate it to a community garden or your favorite Green Thumb. There is always a demand for gorgeous, healthy soil.

Forget Chemical Fertilizers

Chemicals in human-made fertilizers harm and can eventually kill natural microbes in the soil. These include beneficial insects, fungus and bacteria. These naturally occurring critters are actually necessary for healthy soil and plant growth. If nitrogen is absorbed by soil too quickly, it will end up dehydrating and killing the plant. Chemicals in synthetic fertilizers unavoidably leak into the water supply where they can be consumed by wildlife. Connect the dots. Applying chemical fertilizers to any plant you intend to eat means you're saturating the soil they grow in with chemicals to be absorbed. Then after said plant absorbs the chemicals, you pick the plant and eat it.

Meanwhile if you just compost your food scraps and utilize mulch or layered gardening methods, you will have a great supply of natural fertilizer in the black dirt you produce. There will be no harmful by-products and you're keeping stuff out of landfills. Better yet, contact local animal shelters or farms to see if they're getting rid of any chickens, goats, sheep, rabbits or piglets you could adopt and bring into your garden. You'll never think about fertilizer again.

Collect As Much Rainwater As You Can

Do you need public water supply for your swimming pool, flush toilet or to water your lawn? By taking a downspout from your gutter system and inserting it into a 50-, 100-, or 1,000-gallon drum, you can collect enough water from one good rainfall to water everything in your yard the next time things are looking dry. You can hook that water to an outdoor shower setup. You can use that water to flush toilets, run your washing machine or fill your pool. The bigger the rainwater collection bin, the more water you can store. If you don't have gutters on your house, you can put a ten-foot gutter on the side of any shed or garage, hook it to a downspout and collection bin and collect water that way. Even a big wine jug with a funnel sticking out of it on your fire escape in the city will gather enough water for you to take care of your houseplants.

Dig a Pond

Tying into the idea of catching rainwater are ponds. Ponds provide great ecosystems for birds, bugs, fish and frogs. They're water troughs for free-range farm animals. But more than all this, ponds hold water in place. They prevent runoff through suburban neighborhoods and areas with poor soil quality. Ponds allow water to slowly percolate down through the soil, enhancing the biodiversity therein. Ponds can help to raise water tables, recharge aquifers and reduce the amount of water lost to evaporation. If everyone with enough land put in a pond or two on his or her property, water quality and access would improve exponentially.

Eat Your Zip Code and Stop Buying Barcodes

We should all seek food closer to home, in our food shed, our own bioregion. This means enjoying seasonality and reacquainting ourselves with our home kitchens. If you're not pulling it from your backyard, see if you can get it from a neighbor's or at the farmers market over the weekend. The popularity of CSAs and markets like this has made it inexcusable to buy in-season veggies from more than 30 miles away. Anything that has a barcode is a packaged food item. Avoid these as much as humanly possible.

Touch More

Trees you walk by. Grass. Vegetables and fruits. Each other. Touch creates empathy and a sense of connection. A hand on the back. A hug. The soft petals of a flower. Tactile sensation is extremely important for sensory development. It's therapeutic to many of our ills. We don't do enough of it.

Change Your Shopping Habits

The choices you make as a consumer are your most powerful positioning points as a member of this society. Where you put your money will dictate policy, trends, supply and demand. By making small, smart decisions every day about where your food, clothes, house supplies, beauty products and every thing else you pay for comes from, you will be making the biggest impact of all.

Stop Eating So Much Meat

Eighteen percent of what we call the greenhouse effect is believed to be caused by methane, much of which is caused by cud-chewers like sheep, goats, camels, water buffalo and most of all, cattle — of which the world has an estimated 1.2 billion. According to the United Nations, raising animals for food generates more greenhouse gas emissions than all the cars, planes, ships, trucks and trains in the world combined. Seventy percent of the leveled rain forest in the Amazon is used to raise animals for meat consumption.[1] How much of this stuff do we really need to eat?

Try to lessen the amount of meat you consume on a daily basis. Shrink your meat portions when you cook at home. Try out Meatless Mondays or see if you can go a week without. A plant-based diet is a diet of peace: mind, body and soul. If you do buy meat, support the growing number of small farms doing excellent work with crop and animal rotations in pasture. Insist on buying only locally raised organic meats where farmers undertake responsible animal husbandry and holistic management. You should be able to say that the food you consumed — plant or animal — lived a respectable life and was treated fairly. Cleaner, healthier, happier food translates into a better life for you.

This doesn't have to cost you more money. You can often buy a whole pig or a half cow from a local farmer or butcher for significantly less per pound than anything at a supermarket. Do so, and store the meat in a basement freezer. Take a year and don't step foot into any fast-food restaurant. Or a month. Or a week. In addition to the obvious health benefits, you'll be stepping outside the factory-farming chain that has wreaked such havoc on ecosystems, the environment and health.

Honor the Rhythm of the Seasons

Our day-to-day lives defy the natural order of things. We want hot weather when it's cool, light when it's dark, and we want to run our homes the same way 365 days of the year. Stop. Give in to Mother Nature. It's cold outside. Put on a sweater before you raise the thermostat. It's summer. Grow all your own herbs on a windowsill, under a grow light or in your backyard. It's raining. Catch rainwater to irrigate your plants or give water to your pets. It's sunny. Collect solar rays to power your cell phone charger or home electricity. Eat what is in season, and learn how to preserve seasonal food to enjoy during the off-season instead of having it trucked in to your local supermarket. Rest during the winter. Try to spend one day each month without using electricity at home. In the evenings, light candles or lanterns instead of flipping a light switch. If you live in a place that braves hearty winters, explore alternative heat methods utilizing renewables such as pellet or wood stoves. Harness the sun with solar power, underground water temperatures with geothermal or the wind with a turbine or two. Seasonal labor like stacking wood or prepping garden beds will give you a quick education on keeping in lockstep with the weather and seasons.

Cancel Your Gym Membership

Why do we drive to a gym, only to get on a treadmill? Change your habits so that you spend time outside doing active things. Walk or ride your bicycle to work, a friend's house or into town to run a simple errand. Sell your riding mower and get a push mower for your yard. Go dancing instead of to the movies. Take your family hiking, kayaking, roller-skating or cross-country skiing. You'll save a ton of cash and feel more energized.

Stop Throwing Everything Away

Paper towels, plastic cups, plastic straws, cellophane, paper napkins: stop what you are doing! The EPA reported that in 2012 the US generated 32 million tons of plastic waste. Forty billion plastic utensils are used and thrown out every year in just the US, as estimated by Worldcentric.org. And paper products top the charts for waste added to landfills at 27%. To meet demand for plastic water bottles, Americans burn the energy equivalent of 32–54 million barrels of oil each year.[2] So start sporting a handkerchief. Refill your water bottles. Buy some cloth napkins for goodness sake! See if you can go a whole year without using a plastic, throwaway shopping bag. Donate clothing, children's toys and used furniture to thrift shops. Post other items online for sale. And instead of paper towels, cut old clothes and towels into rags to pick up spills and clean house.

Move More

Our bodies were made to move. It's not okay to wake up, drive to work, sit at a desk, drive home and sit on the couch. It's recommended that humans take 10,000 steps in a day, the equivalent of walking five miles. But most people barely crest 2,000. Sedentary lifestyles affect digestion, muscular and skeletal health and make us depressed, lazy and self-absorbed. It's time to do something about this. Among the million reasons a body in motion is good for you is the benefit to your lymph system. This intricate network deals with moving waste from your body — but it doesn't have its own pump. It needs you! Exercise is the pump that will keep the lymph system functioning properly. Get that heart rate up for at least 30 minutes several times a week. Stretch. Bend. It will keep you young and push toxins out of your body.

Don't Put Anything On or In Your Body that You Can't Pronounce

Shampoos, cleaning products, lotions, soaps and food all end up in us, on us and all around us. It's unavoidable. If there's a toxic ingredient in any of the above, it's going to end up in your grey and blackwater systems, backyards and body. The market is saturated with choices. Why not pick the healthiest products you can?

Rescue Some Chickens

Eggs coming out of backyards are healthier for you, better tasting and come from happy birds. The opposite is true for store-bought eggs, even most organic or free-range versions. Many of us have parakeets, cockatiels and parrots as house pets. But not so many of us have chickens. Why? Hens are quieter than other birds, eat your food scraps and lay eggs.

Keeping chickens takes demand off the industrial egg industry, and the birds don't need a whole lot of space. Backyard eggs have approximately 25% more vitamin E, 75% more beta-carotene and as much as 20 times the amount of omega-3 fatty acids as do factory-farmed eggs. Perhaps best of all for those who avoid eating eggs due to worries about cholesterol, backyard eggs contain only about half as much cholesterol as factory-farmed eggs. Every egg factory on Planet Earth is flush with so-called spent hens, hens a year or more older who are no longer at peak egg-production. These companies love to get rid of spent hens!

Call up the closest egg farm you can find and ask if they're getting rid of any. Then go pick them up and show them a loving, heavenly retirement free from overcrowded cages and sad conditions. Our oldest spent-hen rescues have been with us more than three years and still lay eggs almost every day.

Follow the Money

We have bedded down with the idea that junk and fast foods are cheaper than whole foods. In fact it isn't cheaper to eat a highly processed diet: a typical order for a family of four at McDonald's today costs between $20 and $30; while organic veggies, a piece of meat or vegetarian substitute, salad and drink will run you less than $20 and serve up to six. Things get much cheaper if you go the veggies-and-rice route (about $10).[3] This is in spite of the fact that the US government offers millions in subsidies to the sugar, dairy and soy industry. Processed foods are the leading cause of higher health care costs, diabetes, obesity, cancer, heart disease and every other health epidemic we face. How much do such foods cost you over the course of your lifetime? You can eat smaller portions of whole, organic food while gaining more nutrition. The fact is that highly processed foods are across the board pricier than when you prepare whole foods at home — either as up-front costs or as overall, lifetime health care costs. Why not treat that body and this Earth like the temples they are?

Ditch Sugar

The great food conspiracy no one's sharing with you is that the diet game isn't about calories-in, calories-out: it's about sugar. Sugar is made of two molecules: glucose and fructose. Glucose is an essential part of how our bodies make energy, but fructose has little value to our bodies and can't be processed by anything besides the liver. Look on the ingredient list of any low-fat or low-sodium product, cereal, soda, fruit juice or packaged meal. Sugar makes it onto ingredients lists under cover of many names like corn syrup, natural sweeteners or cane juice. What you may not realize is that anytime something is made low-calorie or low-fat, sugar is added to make the food tasty. When we overload our bodies with sugar unaccompanied by fiber to slow down the absorption process, our livers metabolize most of the fructose. Once that happens, the fructose is turned into fat and secreted into the blood. Packaged foods = sugar. Ditch added sugar and you will automatically lose weight, have more energy and see a reduction in common health ailments like headaches. The sugar you do ingest through nuts, fruits and such will have the appropriate amount of fiber to ensure a slow sugar absorption.

Learn to Love to Cook

Too many people view cooking as a burden. Yet cancer rates are through the roof and more than two thirds of people in the US are overweight or obese. What is more burdensome than being sick? Start thinking of your food as your health care. Read up on pH levels in your blood and do all you can — eating lots of fresh veggies and fruit — to keep your blood levels slightly alkaline. Cooking your own food will quickly protect you from the oversaturation of sodium and sugar in store-bought food and keep cancer cells from the acidic environment they need to thrive.

Rethink Your Toilet

Check with your local zoning office about rerouting plumbing to flush your toilets with greywater from your house. Better yet, get over the mindset that toilets need to be flushed. We have no excuse for not pursuing sanitary ways to handle our own excrement without wasting perfectly good drinking water. Our contempt for our own crap is totally out of line with the reality that we too are animals. Compost toilets cost about one tenth that of a new septic system, will provide you with every nutrient you need in your garden and keep millions of gallons of water from being flushed away. And newer models are so sophisticated, by the time you empty the toilet all you're going to find inside is black dirt.

Live Small

Statistically speaking, you're probably living in a home bigger than you need. That means you're overburdening the grid you're hooked to, the fuel you burn, the energy you spend keeping the place clean and lastly, your wallet. Tiny homes are all the rage and can be built for as little as $4,000. All you need is a plot of land or a trailer to get started.

Overcome Your Supermarket Addiction

I know you're busy. I know it's faster to buy granola than make it, simpler to get a loaf of bread than use a bread maker. I get that supermarkets have no seasons, provide one-stop shopping and that we're creatures of habit who have grown accustomed to certain brands, flavors and cooking styles. But in order to get food into supermarkets, growers and suppliers have to jump a bunch of hurdles: insurance requirements, certifications, screenings and fees. Animals must be medicated, vaccinated and free from compost or manure systems. The price we pay for these conveniences harms the natural world, animals and even our own health. So make a change. Switch to using supermarkets only to buy ingredients like baking supplies, bulk items, rice or other grains. Get your produce and meat from your own backyard or local farms. Each summer, preserve some of what you grew by canning or freezing so you can enjoy your own fresh veggies all winter long. The returns on your money and health will embolden you to make this lifestyle change in its entirety. And the deliciousness of the food you're suddenly preparing will inspire the people around you to do the same.

Be Kind

Everyone around you has struggles to work through. So be more patient than you feel, kinder than you want to be and let people be whoever they are. Loving yourself and each other goes hand in hand with being more loving to the world around you. We are all connected.

Stop Making Excuses

Don't say you don't have time to cook for yourself when the average American in 2010 spent just shy of two hours a day watching television. Don't say you can't afford organic food if you still have the money for dinners out, a beer at your favorite watering hole, video games, manicures, a satellite radio subscription or a pack of cigarettes. Instead of finding all the reasons why something can't happen, focus on why something can. For the overwhelming majority of people, it is entirely possible to live healthier, happier and to practice responsible land stewardship. Instead of dreaming up every person for whom this lifestyle shift is impossible, let's talk more about all the people for whom change is possible.

Chapter 12

Start Art Now

One cannot change a habit without changing his or her life.
One cannot change his or her life without changing
the world.

OUR BEHAVIORS AND PERSONALITIES feed off of each other. So we cannot become more mindful of the Earth and more proactive about improving it without also changing our hearts and living more meaningfully. It's time to open ourselves up to allow creativity in. We have to be vulnerable. And we have to stop asking for permission to be great.

In Okinawan culture, *ikigai* is a word that means "a reason for being." Your *ikigai* is your sense of purpose in the world: why you get up in the morning. It's the glitter and gusto that sent Albert Einstein on his way, forced Stanley Kubrick to create and taught Jimi Hendrix how to play guitar. We all possess our own *ikigai*. We only have to tap into it. To achieve this purpose, you're going to need to be armed with extensive soul-searching, a willingness to embrace balance and creativity, a zest for exploration, being in the here and now and perhaps most importantly, openness to chance.

People in the US scramble and claw their way through every day just to make enough money to put food on the table. Working two, three — even four — jobs has become a new normal for many people.

We are all so busy. How can we opt into our artistic lives when we are drowning trying to make ends meet? To get that degree? To make time for the people we love? To make a dollar?

In his book *Ecodeviance: (Soma)tics for the Future Wilderness,* poet CAConrad calls for people to live in the "extreme present" in order to tap into the creative viability all around us. Throughout the text Conrad offers daily rituals that encourage readers to transform their mundane, run-of-the-mill moments and make them magical. Instead of stepping out of your life and trying to overhaul everything at once, Conrad pushes his readers to focus on what is already here. This bird. That security camera. This stranger's arm on mine in a crowded plane. From attempting telepathy with strangers in coffee shop checkout lines to becoming mindful of the sensation of thirst, Conrad's whimsical advice is for us to simply open our eyes as we continue to do our normal routines. And to take notes. To write poetry. To gauge reactions.

Looking at life through a new set of eyes inevitably begins the process of ushering energy and creativity into our living environments. Creativity thrives on the same poisons so many of us wrongly think squash it.

Psychologist Carl Jung was the first to use the terms *synchronicity* and *collective unconscious* to describe spontaneous happenings between otherwise disconnected people or things and the connection all our unconscious minds share. These concepts refer to alchemy: the connection between consciousness and matter.

"For Art's Sake" refers to the act of creating for no other reason than to, indeed, create. So many people are afraid of being wrong, of not being good enough. That is garbage. Many of us in the US get so consumed in the humdrum buzz of daily responsibilities that we forget — between sleep, work, child care and television — to do anything at all that's creative. Yet children inherently seek to create. So what is it that so many of us unlearn somewhere between preadolescence and adulthood?

Somewhere along the line, the system just gives up on young adults. These kids go from wanting to be ballerinas and ball players to mindlessly memorizing answers for a test. We've failed as a culture when we don't encourage young people to be healthy and whole, pursuing their loves and feeding their creativity. We've pushed art to the fringe, only practiced by elites or very young children. Yet art is fundamental to human development. Every child who is handed a crayon, draws.

Here's the thing: the actual act of creating art is good for you emotionally and physically, no matter how old you are. Art therapy has been employed clinically for the last century. But it wasn't until recently that controlled, thorough studies have cohesively illustrated how art affects healing. While US culture is only just getting the proverbial grip on art's importance beyond its aesthetic or audible appeal, history shows that all cultures throughout all of human time have embraced art's ability to promote the healing process in one way or another.

This is an important point to note especially today, in a world where we're bombarded 24/7 by information and entertainment through television, smart phones and the Internet. Many folks in the US live in a reactionary way, just responding to the stimuli around us. Creating art changes that dynamic and makes each individual proactive instead of reactive. The radical act of contributing instead of consuming is a work of art.

Connecting with your inner artist can be as simple as making a homemade card for a loved one or as time-consuming as learning to play a new musical instrument. The point is for it to be something not part of your normal routine; something you do simply for the sake of creation. To tap into your greatest potential, consider the things in the world you consider beautiful. Ask yourself how you would spend your day if money wasn't a concern.

This is how and where you will find your *ikigai*. Whether you're a fisher, farmer, concert pianist, doctor, mason, stay-at-home parent, accountant or baker, tap into the basic part of you that is passionate and turned on by truth and willing to determinedly journey to do now what will make things better later.

We can do all this. One exercise at a time.

Turn on Your Creativity

All the time. Stay open. If someone asks you to make a decision or you have to deal with a trauma, think about the issue from a new angle.

Thinking creatively and being more action-based will make your life feel more like an adventure and less like a struggle.

Savor the Synchronicity of Coincidence

You spent all of yesterday thinking about your best friend from college. Today, he called you. Your inspection sticker was overdue on your car so you delayed a road trip on the same day a horrible blizzard hit and there was a multi-car pileup on the highway. You didn't get your dream job and instead decided to start your own company. Allow for the magical possibility that you can connect to strangers, loved ones, plants and animals. The more you trust the art of synchronicity, the more you're guaranteed to see it at work everywhere.

Doodle

Forget what your teachers told you in high school. Research demonstrates that the act of doodling can help you digest new concepts, learn, think critically and focus. Psychologist Jackie Andrade in 2009 conducted a study published in *Applied Cognitive Psychology* that found people who doodle retain up to 29% more than people who don't.[1] Doodling actually keeps people from daydreaming; so instead of trying to remember everything you have to get done this weekend, you're focused on what you're hearing right now.

Be Here Now

I was over at my sister's place visiting with my amazing nieces Riley and Ella, on Riley's fourth birthday. The girls were sitting at the kitchen table eating oatmeal and drinking juice while we discussed Riley's birthday party coming up that day. In the middle of the planning discussion, Riley smiled and stared at her spoon of oatmeal. "Auntie Coley, eating oatmeal is fun," she said, and laughed. There is so much to learn from children about living in the here and now, and relishing our moments. Eating oatmeal *is* fun. Running a spoon along the side of the bowl, tasting the warm food, smelling the apples and cinnamon or other spices. All of our lives have these spectacular, tiny moments in them. It behooves us all to pay attention.

DIY

Anything done carefully or well is an art. Next time a room in your house needs to be painted, pull out a brush. Replace your own bathtub. Stencil your own wallpaper. Tune up your own bicycle. Draw your own garden map. Wire your own ceiling fan. These little acts will encourage you to use new parts of your brain and will give you a great education in basic home repairs. Call a neighbor who can show you how to do some beginner projects and repay them with a homemade lunch, a ride someplace or help on their computer. The barter system and DIY culture are great alternatives to expensive home repairs and guilt about lack of self-reliance. Once you become relatively handy, your creative juices will be flowing and you'll have a new hobby on your hands.

Practice Mindful Leadership

Mindfulness is non-judgmental awareness. It's an essential skill for entrepreneurs, business owners and leaders in general. When you can be present, people helping you will respect and trust you more. Mindful leadership creates focus, fosters creativity and promotes compassion. The methods of mindful leadership translate from work to home. If you can wake in the morning mindful — of your surroundings, how your sheets feel on your skin, of the colors you see all around you — you will instantly be more connected to the world and people and animals in it.

Make Art

I don't care if you haven't picked up an instrument since being forced to study the recorder in third grade: Each of us has the capacity to make art. Taking adult classes in pottery, photography, creative writing or drumming will expand your social circle and get you out of your own head. Using your time in front of the television to knit, crochet, embroider or collage greeting cards turns idleness into productivity. Try carrying a small notebook in your glove compartment, purse or jacket pocket. Jot down ideas, funny one-liners, quotes or memories.

Prioritize Joyful Activities

When we say we don't have time for something, what we are truly saying is that the activity in question simply isn't a priority. Our choices change when we say things in this way: "I can't make it to your basketball game because it's not a priority for me." Or, "I don't consider this volunteer activity a priority." When you think of this, you realize that we choose every day what we have time for. And in fact, what we set as our priorities are often utterly unimportant things like social media or watching TV. If we prioritize our time and spend it doing things we know bring us joy (tea with a best friend, hiking, sitting in a park eating a picnic lunch), then the time we spend not working acquires added value.

Be Grateful

Consistently grateful people are less stressed and materialistic; they have more energy, compassion, forgiveness and hope.[2] So pay attention to what people do for you every day. Someone holding the door for you at a cafe. A smile from a tollbooth operator. A stranger calling to say she found your wallet. An unexpected phone call from a friend. Look for all the small ways people go out of their way to make your life better. Thank them.

Upcycle

Make a mosaic out of cracked tiles. Turn a feedbag into a purse. Make throw pillow covers out of your old concert T-shirts. Make a lamp out of a log, bottle or sculpture. Reimagine that which seems irrelevant. There is so much meaning to be found in this practice.

Let Your Grief Inspire You

Newsflash: Your life is going to fall apart. But what you do with the pieces will define you.

Part 3

Let the beauty we love be what we do.
There are hundreds of ways to kneel and
kiss the ground.

— Jalāl ad-Dīn Muhammad Rūmī

Do It Yourself!

T HERE YOU ARE! You're waking up. Once bitten (no longer shy) by the teeth of freedom. The whole world's alive. There is much to do. Let the fun begin!

So you've read the book, you're hip to the theory and you know change is coming. You've lit the match and are shifting your perspectives in order to recreate the world around you. You're enjoying a sense

AmberLee Clement and Kathryn Mollica work on a construction project at Better Farm in 2013. CREDIT: NICOLE CALDWELL

Sustainability students in 2012 designed a comic, foreground roadside attraction at Better Farm. CREDIT: NICOLE CALDWELL

of whimsy. You're seeking out coincidences. You're ready to get creative.

Now you'll need a few tools. This section of *Better* will arm you with full instructions for making your life your greatest artistic achievement and start you on the road to a healthier, happier life.

This Part of *Better* includes instructions to:

> Create Your Own Aquaponics Tank
> Upcycle Every Day
> Collect Rainwater
> Create DIY Stencils
> Cultivate a Basic Garden for a Family of Four
> Build a Starter Chicken Coop
> Set Up Your Own Compost Bin
> Turn Old Windows into a Greenhouse or Cold Frame
> Create a Basic Greywater Filtration System
> Execute Small Space Gardening

Aquaponics: Turn Your Fish Tank into a Garden

Growing plants in an aquaponics setup is one of the most passive, cheapest and easiest ways to cultivate food. The fish, water pump and light timer do all the work — all you have to do is feed the fish in the morning and harvest your produce. Costs range from less than $50 for a tiny kitchen counter setup, to around $400 for a large kit (if you're willing to upcycle and buy second-hand). If you tally up what you spend in a year on salad greens and herbs, you're likely to find this mini-farm is a safer investment than the stock market any day of the week. While the materials list is a bit daunting, the process is anything but.

MATERIALS

- Fish tank (at least 40 gallons if you want to raise edible fish)
- Fish tank filter system (two corner filters to circulate the water)
- Gravel for the bottom of the tank
- Grow bed for plants (as basic as any watertight container or as complex as an industrial planting bed from a gardening store — should be large enough to sit on top of your fish tank)

Basic Aquaponics Schematic.
CREDIT:
NICOLE CALDWELL

- Water pump (the smallest pond pump you can find and compatible clear tubing to run from the pump to the grow bed — at Better Farm we use ½-inch tubing cut to appropriate length)
- Pea gravel (for grow bed)
- Fluorescent grow light
- Stand for fluorescent light (or build your own)
- Light timer (optional)
- Fish (start with feeder fish or minnows then switch to edible fish like tilapia, trout, carp or largemouth bass once pH is set)
- pH test kit
- Nitrogen test kit
- Seeds (easiest for aquaponics newbies are salad greens and herbs)

INSTRUCTIONS

1. Set up your tank (not your grow bed yet!) with gravel in the bottom, a few cool places for fish to hang out like castles or water plants, and add water. Let the tank circulate for two to four days (especially if you are drawing from treated, public water); this will allow chemicals like chlorine to work their way out of the system and will ensure your gravel is thoroughly clean.

2. After several days, add fish. The golden rule of aquariums is one inch of fish for every gallon of water you have. Remember that fish will grow! Some of the fish will inevitably die. When they do, leave them floating in the water. As the feeder fish break down, they'll become ammonia-based waste. Bacteria will slowly colonize and turn ammonia into nitrite (ammonia and nitrite are both toxic to plants). After that, more bacteria will colonize and change nitrite into nitrate, which is usable fertilizer for your grow bed.

3. Let the system grow into itself. Execute weekly nitrogen and pH tests until everything is optimal (40–80 ppm for nitrogen levels; pH can vary depending on what kind of fish you have in the tank).

4. While this is happening, set up your grow bed. Place the container flat on top of the fish tank, then prop up one end with a piece of wood (1x1 inch or 2x2 inches is fine) to allow gravity to pull water across the bed. At the low end, drill many holes through

the container to allow water to drain. Fill the container with many smaller plastic pots of pea gravel (this will make for easier cleaning), or fill the entire container with about six inches of pea gravel.

5. Set up the light. If your light didn't come with a stand, build a basic box frame out of scrap wood and secure it to the surface supporting the fish tank.

6. Hook up the water pump and tubing. The lower in the tank the better for the pump — the most ammonia is at the bottom! Make sure you have enough tubing to get from the pump all the way up to the highest part of your grow bed. Turn the pump on, adjust the speed of your pump accordingly, and let the whole system run for 24 to 48 hours in order to troubleshoot any issues.

7. Plant your seeds. For salad greens, simply sprinkle the seeds evenly over the pea gravel in your grow bed. For other plants such as tomatoes, proper spacing (and regular trimming!) will be necessary.

8. As a standard rule for most plants, you should have your grow light on for 12 hours, off for 12 hours. As you progress and want to experiment with blooming or fruiting plants, lighting will have to be adjusted accordingly.

9. Feed your fish daily, keeping in mind that a healthy fish will consume around 1.5 percent of his or her body weight each day. Do not overfeed!

10. Check your pH and nitrogen levels monthly.

11. Clean your filtration system and tubing regularly. Most tank filters recommend monthly cleanings, however you will find with all the filtration happening in your grow bed (and with appropriate feeding levels for your fish) that you will only need to clean out your system twice a year.

12. When plants appear, trim or harvest them as needed for each individual plant type. Salad greens can be harvested with a pair of scissors. Leaving the roots intact will allow new vegetation to grow.

Everyday Upcycling

Upcycling breathes new life into old stuff, keeps things out of the landfill, beautifies your home and garden, teaches you new skills and encourages you to tap into your creativity. What follow are a few tutorials for some of the most common skills you'll need to repurpose old things into new.

Sustainability student Allison Bachner upcycled a shelf with newspaper, paint and elbow grease in 2014.
Credit: Nicole Caldwell

betterArts board member Holly Boname poses under an upcycled hair dryer created by artist-in-residence Mike Brown. Credit: Nicole Caldwell

Basic Sewing

MATERIALS

- Thread
- Scissors
- Fabric to sew
- Sewing needle (various sizes depend on size of project)

INSTRUCTIONS

1. Cut about an arm's length of thread and put one end through the eye of the needle.
2. Make several knots one on top of another at the other end of the thread so the thread stops when the end reaches the fabric.
3. Turn the fabric inside out so you will not see your seams or leave any exposed, rough edges.
4. Push the needle through the fabric in desired location and pull the thread through until the knot catches it.
5. Put the needle back through the fabric where it came out. Keep your stitches small, less than an inch at all times.
6. Continue sewing until you run almost out of thread on the needle. Tie two knots in the string by bringing your needle under and around your last stitch.
7. Unroll more thread and continue until done.

Basic Embroidery

MATERIALS

- Embroidery hoop
- Embroidery needle
- Embroidery floss
- Fabric
- Pencil to make design, or ready-made template

A Basic Satin Stitch. CREDIT: NICOLE CALDWELL

INSTRUCTIONS

1. With pencil, sketch out a basic design on the fabric you would like to embroider. This works best on fabric that hasn't been stitched together yet, but you can certainly embroider pillowcases, sheets, shirts and more. If you have a store-bought template, apply it now.
2. Put your fabric between the top and bottom parts of the embroidery hoop and screw shut tightly so the fabric doesn't slide while you make your stitches.

> There are some easy embroidery stitches that will make any beginner seem like a master. For either of these starter stitches, remember to first make a knot on the back of your embroidery, either by tying several knots at one end of the floss or by putting your needle through the fabric twice and making a double knot on the back of your fabric.

Backstitch —- This stitch is perfect for outlining, especially for basic drawings you want to make with floss. The finished product will look like a dotted line.

CREDIT: NICOLE CALDWELL

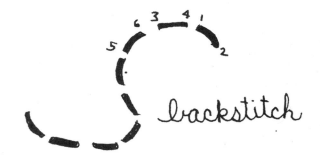

1. Thread your needle with floss. Come up through the fabric from behind and go back down to make your first stitch.
2. For your second stitch, back up to a stitch length away from your first, then come back down right next to it.
3. Continue backing across your fabric this way to create an outline. You can set your own distance between stitches however you like, just be consistent!

satin stitch

Satin Stitch — The satin stitch creates a solid band of color that is lovely and smooth like satin. I love using the satin stitch to write words, but it's also a great stitch for flower petals and trees.

CREDIT: NICOLE CALDWELL

1. Thread your needle with floss. Come up from back to front of fabric, go back down.
2. When you come back through the fabric for your next stitch, go back to the top where you started your first stitch. You want each stitch to go from top to bottom in order to keep the thread perfectly straight. You are essentially creating loops of floss over the fabric.

Basic Wiring — DIY Lamp

You can make a lamp out of just about anything: a tree trunk, bottle, sculpture, figurines or even a pile of books.

MATERIALS

- Lamp kit (or bought separately: bolts, cord set, detachable harp, finial, nuts, push-through socket and socket shell, rod and washers)
- Lamp base (the object to be turned into a lamp)
- Light bulb
- Hole saw cutter or spade drill bit for making hole in base for lamp
- Drill
- Wire strippers or knife
- Lampshade with mount
- Screwdriver

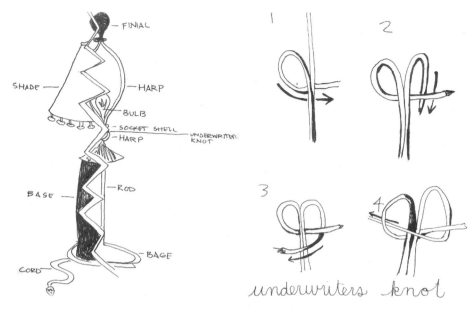

Basic Lamp-Wiring Schematic.

CREDIT: NICOLE CALDWELL

Underwriter's Knot. CREDIT: NICOLE CALDWELL

INSTRUCTIONS

1. Drill a hole through your base wide enough for the wire and rod to pass through. If your base is long, you may need a special drill bit that will do the job.
2. Stabilize the base. Rubber washers stuck to the bottom will work to prevent sliding and make room for the cord to come out from under the base.
3. Attach your rod to the base. Secure with nut and washer.
4. Thread the cord through your lamp base and rod from bottom to top, leaving at least three inches of cord sticking out the top.
5. When you have the cord where you want it, screw the lock nut onto the top of the lamp rod.
6. Add the harp bottom to the top of the lamp rod.
7. Screw the socket cap, opening facing up, to the harp bottom.
8. Pull the covered wires at the top of the cord apart about four inches and strip the first inch using wire strippers or a knife.

9. Tie the split wires into an underwriter's knot (see diagram) to keep wires from falling through the rod to the base.

10. Wrap the wires around the screws on the bulb socket. The white wire is neutral and the black is hot. If your wires aren't colored, you can pick the neutral one out by its ribbed insulation or by consulting the lamp kit instructions. The bulb socket will have two screws in different colors. The neutral wire goes clockwise around the silver or white screw; the hot wire goes clockwise around the gold or dark screw.

11. Tighten the screws down with a screwdriver.

12. Fit the socket shell down over the bulb socket, lining up the switch and socket shell, and press into place. Cords should be tucked inside out of view.

13. Attach the top of the harp and lampshade.

14. Screw in a light bulb and plug in your new lamp!

Once you have these basic skills down, you can go wild finding new lives for old things. For example:

Repurposed Planters

- Old shoes — Apply outdoor acrylic sealer to outside and inside of shoes, then choose plants with shallow roots.
- Claw tubs — Use a power sander to remove old paint from outside and spray paint any color of your choice.
- Metal buckets — Just drill holes in the bottom and fill!
- 50-gallon plastic drums — Saw in half, drill holes in the bottom of each and paint the outside.
- Birdcage — Spray paint and add a potted plant. If birdcage has a solid floor, fill the bottom with dirt and plant directly into that.
- Pallet —
  1. Cut pallet down to desired size.
  2. Cut a piece of landscape fabric four or five inches longer and wider than pallet, and staple along back and three sides of pallet so no dirt spills out (leave the side that will be the top open so you can plant into it).
  3. Pack the pallet with dirt, and plant from bottom to top.

4. Water and let plants settle for a week or two before mounting the planter to an inside or outside wall.

Homemade Lighting Fixtures

- Driftwood, sculptural and bottle lamps
- Wagon wheel, mason jar or wire-bowl chandeliers

Furniture

- Revive your old wood furniture — Swapping out hardware on cabinetry or drawers, stripping, distressing and painting will breathe new life into old furniture at home.

Make a mosaic tabletop, backsplash or coaster

Textiles

- Repurposed T-shirts as tote bags, pillow case covers or quilts
- Chicken feed bags upcycled as reusable shopping bags
- Homemade curtains, skirts

Wall Art

Turn old wood frames into outdoor pieces of art by stapling on a canvas of your choosing to it and adding sections of window screen, landscape cloth, leaves, burlap and paint.

Collect Rainwater

Rainwater harvesting is the ancient practice of catching and storing water that runs off hardscapes for later use. Rainwater captured in barrels, cisterns and ponds can be used for everything from outdoor showers to irrigation. Designs for catchment systems range from extremely simple to highly complex. At its most basic, rainwater catchment is achieved with a simple gutter attached to a roofline, with a downspout that enters a large plastic drum. A spigot at the bottom of the drum allows for a gravity-fed water line to be hooked to a hose or showerhead.

Rainwater collected in this method for a shower will require keeping the barrel high enough to stand under, or investing in a small pump to run water from the barrel into an overhead shower spigot. To use collected water for an outdoor sink, put the barrel up at table level and have the spigot shoot water directly into the sink. At Better Farm, we use a rainwater collection system next to the art studio as a station for washing hands and brushes while two catchment systems next to the garden are for irrigation of plants outside and in the greenhouses. There are many variations of rainwater catchment, but here's a basic setup to get you started.

MATERIALS

- Gutter to run length of roofline
- Downspout to connect from gutter to barrel
- Two end caps for gutter
- Gutter drop outlet that connects gutter to downspout
- Brackets to hold up the gutter against house, shed or garage
- Galvanized screws

Sustainability students complete a rainwater catchment barrel system in 2012.

CREDIT: NICOLE CALDWELL

- Barrel (50-gallon is most universal, but you can buy much larger or smaller or get used ones from local farmers; just be sure to thoroughly clean any hand-me-downs)
- Base for barrel (cinder blocks at least for a hose attachment, something taller if you want a sink; you are using gravity to pull the water from the barrel into your spigot, which should be at the bottom of the barrel!)
- Spigot for barrel
- Two washers for spigot
- Mosquito screen (metal screen or mesh with tiny openings) for opening at top of barrel to ensure no bugs lay eggs in the water
- Some way to attach mosquito screen to barrel: staples, screws or waterproof adhesive will work
- Drill with various bits: one to fit your screws, one with a drill head of the same diameter as your spigot
- Jig saw to cut a hole in your barrel for the downspout

INSTRUCTIONS

1. Mark a square opening on the top of your barrel about 4x4 inches for where the downspout will enter the barrel. Drill a hole somewhere inside the square to allow a starting point for your jig saw. Use the jig saw to trace the lines of the opening for the downspout.
2. Mark an x on the front of the barrel three inches from the bottom for the spigot. Use your drill to cut a hole in the barrel's side where you have marked the x.
3. Set your barrel up on a base sturdy enough that it will not collapse or rot. The gutter will be cut and attached to the roof, and the downspout will lead directly into the rainwater barrel.
4. Put a washer on your spigot and screw it into the hole in the barrel.
5. Measure your roof edge and cut your gutter length to fit (any saw will be able to cut through plastic gutter).
6. Take your gutter braces and screw them along the roofline, ensuring a gradual angle so the water runs downstream to where your catchment barrel is waiting.

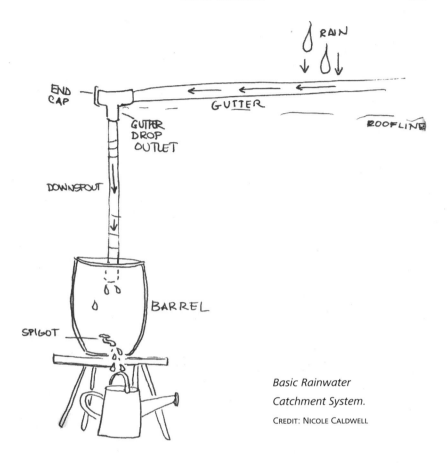

*Basic Rainwater
Catchment System.*
Credit: Nicole Caldwell

7. Put your gutter in the braces and attach downspout attachment piece to the lower end.
8. Attach endcaps.
9. Measure from the gutter to the top of where your barrel sits and cut your downspout to be just a few inches longer.
10. Attach the downspout to the downspout attachment piece of the gutter system, making sure the bottom of it is inside the top of the barrel.
11. Attach mosquito screen around top opening of barrel, working around the downspout's entrance point. Secure with staples, screws or waterproof adhesive.

Create DIY Stencils

Homemade stencils have hundreds of applications, but can most commonly be used to make your own gift wrap, beautify walls of your home without having to mess around with wallpaper or decorate fabric to be turned into clothes or upholstery.

MATERIALS

- Stencil sheet — while you can use cardboard or construction paper to make a stencil, clear acetate is more durable and not terribly expensive from craft supply stores. It's also the easiest way to transfer an image onto your stencil. In a pinch, plastic book-report covers work too.
- Short, sharp utility knife
- Tape
- Stencil image

INSTRUCTIONS

1. Pick a stencil image or draw your own.
2. Tape a printout of the image onto the back of your stencil sheet.
3. Trace the outline of the image on the stencil sheet with your knife. Have something underneath that can bear the scratch marks, like an old piece of wood or multiple layers of cardboard.
4. Remove the image from the back of your stencil.

Stenciled Better Farm Beverage Cozies. CREDIT: NICOLE CALDWELL

Homemade "Better" Stencil. CREDIT: NICOLE CALDWELL

5. To use your stencil, affix it over the medium you're going to design. You can use a foam brush, roller, spray paint or even colored pencils or crayons to color in your stencil.

Cultivate a Basic Garden for a Family of Four

For all of you starting in with the backbreaking work of tilling, weeding, fertilizing and otherwise prepping your garden beds for the impending season, STOP WHAT YOU ARE DOING!

Turn off that rototiller. Back away from that hoe. Return that bag of fertilizer. Pronto.

Mulch gardening will make your soil healthy, prolific and lovable — and will save you a ton of time over the course of the growing season by reducing weeds, nourishing plants and retaining water. The designs for mulch gardening can be adjusted according to how much space you have — although you'll be surprised by how little space you need. Whether you have great soil or are using raised beds, mulch gardening is a perfect way to incorporate compost into the growing process and to recycle your old junk mail, cardboard and other paper packaging. Mulching will also work for any potted plants!

Ideally, you will start a mulch garden outside six months or even a year before you expect to use it. If however you are as impatient as I am and are establishing a mulch garden within the same few months you expect to plant (and for potted plants), be sure to add a thick top layer of good soil. This will ensure your plants have all the things they need while the layers below break down and turn into yummy food for all your plants.

Better Farm's Mulch Garden. CREDIT: NICOLE CALDWELL

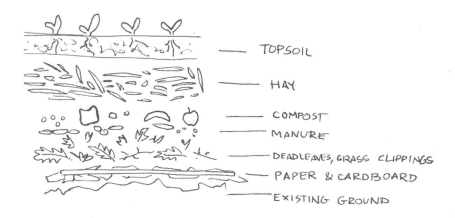

TOPSOIL

HAY

COMPOST

MANURE

DEADLEAVES, GRASS CLIPPINGS

PAPER & CARDBOARD

EXISTING GROUND

The Basic Mechanics of Mulch Gardening. CREDIT: NICOLE CALDWELL

MATERIALS

- Optional: wood or composite to build raised beds (if you build raised beds, don't make them more than three feet wide — you need to be able to reach across them)

Rows of Mulch Gardening at Better Farm. CREDIT: NICOLE CALDWELL

Mulch Garden Results at Better Farm. CREDIT: NICOLE CALDWELL

- Trowel
- Junk mail, cardboard, newspaper, brown paper bags
- Compost (can be new or old)
- Dead leaves, twigs, logs
- Hay (the older and more rotten the better, which also makes it easy to get for F-R-E-E)
- Seeds (ask your family to list their favorite fruits and veggies and grow them)
- Paper and pen to map your garden

INSTRUCTIONS

1. Draw a map of how you want your garden to look. Mark it to scale (one inch=one foot) and indicate where raised beds, rows or semi-circles will go. Even if your garden will be a few containers on your back deck, draw the design out. Also mark where you will be planting what. Companion planting guides online can help you determine what plants do well next to each other. You can return to these drawings year after year in order to keep track of plant rotation.

2. Lay your cardboard and other paper products down on the ground (or in the bottom of your container). This forms a weed barrier and helps with water retention. This layer will eventually decompose and help with the compost ratio.

3. Next, add a layer of dead leaves, grass clippings, compost, several-years-old composted manure and other biodegradables such as old hay. Mulch gardening can range from just a few inches thick to two feet or more, depending on how bad your soil is and how much raw material you have available. Everything you mulch will eventually cook down and settle quite a bit.

    Our layers at Better Farm are about a foot thick, with a fresh layer of cardboard placed over the top as everything breaks down and we see evidence of emerging weeds. We add hay regularly around our plants as they grow to provide them with plenty of mulch. The cyclical process goes on year-round and works so well we don't have to put a single additive or chemical into the soil.

If you are starting this process in the fall, you can leave these layers to cook down over the winter. By spring, you will be able to plant directly into these layers. Variations on layers include adding dirt and/or woodchips to the top layer for aesthetic reasons and to provide additional footholds and mulch for your plants as they grow. If you are starting the mulch garden in the spring, add a scoop of dirt in each spot you'll be planting a seed or transplanting a seedling.

This system will give you a major break in manual irrigation, as the mulch gardening method retains moisture and offers temperature control to plants. Even during droughts, we can stick our finger into the mulch layers at Better Farm and feel damp soil.

4. Keep adding. You can sprinkle compost around each plant if you have good protection in your garden from critters (otherwise use a protected composter and only add freshly formed dirt around plants). Invest in a paper shredder and add cut-up junk mail, newspapers and more around plants as mulch. Throughout and after each season, load your garden rows or beds up with hay — we try to add several feet of hay to our rows every fall. This provides the added benefit of extending your growing season by offering plants great insulation.

Build a Starter Chicken Coop

All chickens need in order to be happy and healthy is a clean place to sleep that's wind-, rain- and predator-proof. Your coop can have as many fancy add-ons as you like once you have those basics covered. Those of you just starting out with a few birds will have no problem building a starter coop for next-to-nothing, as what you already have in scrap lumber and other materials (or what you can get from friends' workshops or the local dump) is likely all you need.

As a general rule, it's a good idea to get a chicken coop up off the ground so predators like raccoons can't scratch through the walls over the course of a night. The bottom of where the birds sleep should ideally be at least three feet off the ground. These plans should be modified according to the materials you have, but they will give you a general structure for putting together a simple coop your birds will love.

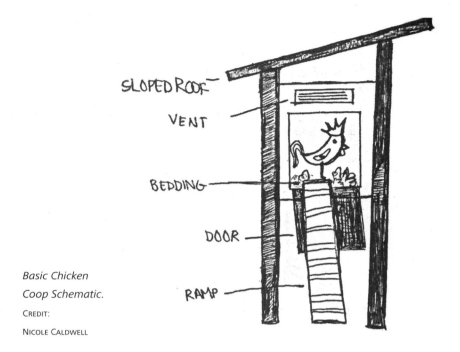

SLOPED ROOF

VENT

BEDDING

DOOR

RAMP

*Basic Chicken
Coop Schematic.*
CREDIT:
NICOLE CALDWELL

If your birds are going to be penned in, pick up a roll of chicken wire at the local hardware store and use garden stakes to cordon off an area in front of your coop. It's always best to keep your coop mobile so you can move the paddock to ensure a fresh supply of greens and bugs as the birds turn the ground over. The dirt they leave behind is a great place to start garden beds, which is why many people opt to use the paddock system inside their garden spaces.

MATERIALS

- Plywood in several sizes for walls
- Four 2x6s for small coop, or four 4x4s for large coop (these will be your corners and legs)
- 2x4s for framing
- 1x6 for ramp
- Roofing material
- Chicken wire

- Hinges (at least two)
- Handle for doors
- Metal wall vent
- Drill
- Circular saw
- Measuring tape
- Galvanized screws
- Hay or shredded paper for nesting material
- Cardboard for lining the bottom of coop
- Spray foam insulation in a can for seams
- Branches at least three inches in diameter for perches

INSTRUCTIONS

1. Measure your largest pieces of plywood. You will need six pieces for your sides, floor and roof. Make a drawing of how you want the coop to look.
2. Build your frame. Corner posts should run from the ground to the top of the coop, connected along perimeter of ceiling and floor by 2x4s wrapping the outside.
3. Cut plywood for walls, floor and roof. You will have to notch the corners of floor and ceiling to fit inside corner posts. Roof should overhang the sides by several inches all around. A hole will have to be cut near the top of one of the walls for the vent, as well. Do not attach walls yet!
4. Cut out a square of plywood on your front wall two inches up from the bottom on center to make an exit door for the chickens. Make sure the door is large enough for you to reach inside for egg retrieval and coop cleaning.
5. Attach hinge at bottom of door, screw a chunk of wood scrap to the front wall just above the top opening of the door to create a turnable stop at night when you close the birds in.
6. Screw walls, floor and ceiling to frame.
7. Add weatherproofing to roof. Use scrap metal roofing, discarded shingles or even cut aluminum cans into overlapping shapes and fasten pieces down with screws or a staple gun.

8. If box is large enough, add one-foot partitions in the back of the box for nesting and a couple of perches.
9. Make ramp. Cut 1x6 so it comes off the ground at an angle and catches the lip of the box when the door is open. Every four inches, screw horizontal strips of 1x6 to give birds traction when walking in and out of the coop.
10. Line the coop with cardboard and add a thick layer of dry hay or paper shreds throughout. This can be replaced weekly; dirtied cardboard and bedding can be added to garden rows or composter.
11. Add your birds to the coop after sunset and close the door. In the morning, let them out, feed and water them as usual. Most birds will return to the coop the next night on their own.

The Art of Compost

Consider growing your own food your civic duty and composting as your radical act. Done properly, you'll be creating your own closed-loop food production system that flies in the face of Big Ag. There are only two things you need for a basic compost setup: a small container in your kitchen to catch food scraps (you can buy an actual compost container with venting or simply use any jar, vase or container with lid) and a larger bin outside to store them.

Composting is the simplest, most natural thing in the world. It doesn't require tumblers or bins that can cost you hundreds of dollars. With a few wood pallets, a drill and outdoor decking screws, you can have a three-tier compost bin in less than 15 minutes that will last for years and provide you with a rotating supply of gorgeous, black dirt. A homemade tumbler next to your garden can turn food scraps to dirt in a matter of weeks under perfect conditions. If you're in a city and/or don't have a yard, vermicompost is the way to go. You'll just need a large waterproof container under your sink to hold the worms. Done right, your guests — and pests like bugs/rats/mice — will never know the worms and food scraps are there!

Compost this: Fruits, vegetables, eggshells, coffee grounds and filters, tea bags, nut shells, shredded newspaper, cardboard, paper, grass

This three-tier compost station in Redwood, New York, was built by volunteers from the Redwood Neighborhood Association and Better Farm. CREDIT: NICOLE CALDWELL

clippings, houseplants, hay and straw, leaves, sawdust, wood chips, cotton and wool rags, dryer and vacuum cleaner lint, hair, fur and fireplace ashes.

Wastes which will attract pests and produce odors: Dairy, eggs and meat products, oils, greases and pet wastes (you can still compost all of these, but additional precautions like sturdy pest barriers are necessary).

Three-Tier Outdoor Compost Bin

All your dead leaves, grass clippings, twigs, hay and kitchen food scraps get tossed into the first section of your compost bin until it's a full, big pile. When that bin is full, you shovel it all into the second bin (top-to-bottom). Then you go back to filling the first section all over again. When compartment #1 fills up again, you move everything from compartment #2 to #3, and from #1 to #2. Then you start over. When all three compartments are full (this should take the average household a full year or even longer), the third bin should be ready to be shoveled out into your garden.

Over time, the materials in each bin will be decomposing. The process is sped up by turning (manually shoveling the pile into the next bin), rainwater falling from overhead and the natural aeration that occurs when oxygen reaches your pile from the nice big spaces between the wood of the pallets. Also, because you're leaving a bare earth floor, worms and other bugs have easy access to your compost heap.

If you're worried about backyard pests like raccoons or coyotes, be sure to install fronts onto the three sections of your compost bin. And of course, if you live in suburbs or the city, you may be subject to zoning or community board laws that would require a closed compost container such as a tumbler. For the rest of you, here's how to have your own three-tier compost bin in quickly and for just the cost of screws.

MATERIALS

- Pallets (12 feet of pallets for back wall, four 4-foot pallets for the walls. Check with your local hardware store, contractors, big box stores, or your local transfer station. Free pallets are in abundance!)
- Galvanized decking screws (longer is better)
- Optional: Three front doors for your compost sections with hinges (each door should measure 4x4 feet)

INSTRUCTIONS

1. Screw the far left wall into the back wall with screws every six inches or so, driven from back to front.
2. Repeat with the second wall (if pallet is wide enough, screw it into both sections of back wall. If not, you may need some additional pieces of wood to create a solid back to screw into. We were fortunate enough to find a very long pallet to have one continuous back wall).
3. Continue until you have four walls and one solid back wall.

Outdoor Compost Tumbler

An outdoor compost tumbler will allow you to make compost fast by aerating your decomposing materials so they break down more quickly than by sitting in a pile. Store-bought tumblers are tough to find for

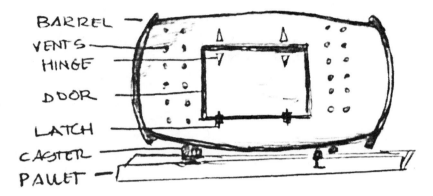

Basic Design for Turning a Plastic Barrel into a Compost Tumbler.

CREDIT: NICOLE CALDWELL

less than $100; luckily, a homemade model will only run you the cost of items you can't readily find around your garage for free.

MATERIALS

- 50-gallon plastic drum (free ones abound at local works yards, transfer stations and farms)
- Six ½-inch rubber washers
- Four medium-sized rolling casters
- Three ½-inch x 4 foot PVC pipes
- Two latches
- Two hinges
- Short galvanized screws to fit latches and hinges
- One pallet (check with your local hardware or feed store, mason or transfer station)
- Drill
- Jig saw
- Permanent marker

INSTRUCTIONS

1. Mark a door opening on the side of your barrel. The opening should be large enough to allow a shovel in for dumping yard debris.

2. With your drill and a spade bit, make a hole in each corner of the marked door for the jig saw.
3. Use the jig saw to trace the lines and cut the door opening.
4. Mark where your hinges and latch will go, then attach them.
5. Create aeration by making holes with your drill about the size of a marble all over the barrel.
6. Make tumblers to help break up all your biodegradables. Use a half-inch drill bit to make three holes in each end of the barrel. Run your PVC lengths through the holes from one end to the other and secure with rubber washers.
7. Make your compost tumbler stand. The easiest and fastest thing you can do is use a pallet. You just need a surface that you can attach casters to so the barrel can be rolled in place while sitting on top of the pallet.
8. To figure out where to attach casters, lay the barrel on its side over your stand and mark where you want the casters to hit to allow the barrel to easily roll.
9. Attach your casters.
10. Add compost!

Indoor Vermicompost Bin

Composting with worms requires six to seven inches of bedding. One gallon of worms need about a square foot of space, keeping in mind the worms reproduce and will need to expand. At the end of the vermicomposting cycle more bins will be necessary to accommodate the growing worm population. Or, pass the additional worms along to your community garden, local farmer or gardener friend. Keep your bin under your kitchen sink where it is nice and dark — worms hate light! This will also keep the bin out of sight.

MATERIALS

- Red wriggler worms (yes, you can buy them online and yes, they are worth every penny)
- Sturdy waterproof container (not translucent) with lid
- Lots of shredded paper (e.g. newspapers, magazines)

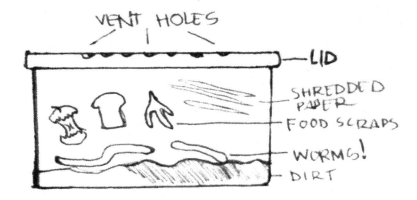

All You Need for Your Own Vermicompost Bin. Credit: Nicole Caldwell

- Food scraps
- Drill with small bit to make holes in top of container
- Cloth to lay over the top of bin

Instructions

1. Drill several holes in the lid of your container so the worms will have access to air.
2. Soak the shredded paper, then wring dry. There should be enough paper to spread six to seven inches of bedding across the bottom of the container.
3. Throw some produce scraps on the paper so bacteria can begin to propagate before the worms are introduced (worms love bacteria).
4. Add the worms and close the container.
5. Wet the cloth, wring it out and lay it over the top of the compost bin. This will help keep the bedding moist and will keep flies or other small bugs out of the bin.

At the first sign of unpleasant odors coming from your vermicompost bin, you can:

1. Mix your compost to aerate the goodies inside.
2. Neutralize the pH with carbon-rich browns (straw, dried leaves or shredded newspaper).

3. Chop your food scraps into smaller pieces before adding to bin. This helps the worms break it down faster.

As your worms start producing dirt, you can scoop out the composted material and add it directly to your houseplants, garden rows or bag it up as topsoil next season. If you don't want to lose your worms in the process, sift dirt into a secondary container through a screen with holes big enough for dirt but not big enough for worms to pass through.

Turn Old Windows into a Greenhouse or Cold Frame

Extending your growing season for fresh produce will feed you year round, offer you streams of income and can even heat your home. Any

This greenhouse at Better Farm was constructed out of discarded windows donated by neighbors. CREDIT: NICOLE CALDWELL

Inside Better Farm's Windowed Greenhouse. CREDIT: NICOLE CALDWELL

house can add a south-facing greenhouse to an exterior wall to provide a passive heat source that could heat your home, a hot tub or even a swimming pool. Free-standing greenhouse structures double as storage for garden tools and can be turned into a chicken coop in the winter months (the birds will heat things up for your plants, which you'll want to protect in cold frames from the birds). Plans can get pretty high-tech — so we'll start small with a basic greenhouse you can build out of windows, and a tiny cold frame that requires only one window and a few pieces of scrap wood.

Basic Window Greenhouse Project

Only your imagination and the windows you end up with limit the size of your greenhouse and its actual design.

MATERIALS

- Discarded windows
- 2x4s
- Four 4x4s
- Greenhouse plastic or corrugated, clear plastic for roof
- Galvanized screws
- Door
- Drill

INSTRUCTIONS

1. Measure all your windows and lay them out on the ground so you can see them.
2. Create a pattern of windows for each wall, adhering to a basic framework for the finished product (10x10 is a good size for a seedling greenhouse that will also store your gardening equipment).
3. Build a frame for each wall of windows. Use 2x4s to make all the studs, with 4x4s for your corners. If your greenhouse is going to be larger than 10x10, you will need to pour cement footers to brace your 4x4s. If you want to get around certain annoying zoning laws, just bury cinder blocks on their sides and slide your 4x4s into them. Be sure to frame in an opening for your door!

4. Pick up each framed wall of the greenhouse and brace.
5. Screw the windows onto the frame, hinging a window or two on each wall for ventilation. If/when a window breaks, it will be easy to unscrew the one to be replaced.
6. Hang your door.
7. Leave the floor earthen or pour in gravel.
8. Build your roof. Depending on what material you are using and where you live, you will want at least a four-degree pitch.

Cold Frame

A cold frame is a boxed enclosure with a transparent roof and no floor. It's basically a mini greenhouse that can be moved around and placed over any plant of your choosing to extend or get a jump start on the growing season. Cold frames are unbelievably easy to make using just a few pieces of scrap wood, an old window, some nails, hinges and a few power tools.

MATERIALS

- One old window (ask neighbors or check your garage)
- Two hinges

Basic Cold Frame Schematic. CREDIT: NICOLE CALDWELL

- Wood to use for the front, back, sides and braces (2x10 is best, but use what you have)
- Galvanized screws
- Drill
- Circular saw

INSTRUCTIONS

1. Cut wood into four pieces matching the length and width of the window. If you are using boards smaller than 2x10, you may have to connect two side-by-side with a furring strip in order to give your cold frame the proper height for your plants.
2. Connect all your sides, bracing corners by putting vertical pieces of 2x4 or other scrap wood inside each corner to screw into.
3. Attach a hinge at each end of one of the window's longest sides.
4. Attach window to frame with hinge.
5. If you're comfortable with basic carpentry, try making the back wall of your cold frame higher than the front to allow more light in.

Greywater Filtration System

Greywater is water that's been used in washing machines, dishwashers, kitchen sinks and showers: just about any water used except in the toilet (that is called blackwater and obviously contains far more contaminants). It is not necessary to add greywater to existing septic tanks; in fact, greywater can be filtered and reused for irrigation, flushing toilets or recycled back through the laundry system.

This method of reuse is called *stacking functions* in the permaculture community. It's simple enough for us to all to be utilizing some version of stacking functions in our homes and businesses.

Food for thought: The average garden in the burbs requires up to 3,000 gallons of water each month. Coincidentally, the average family of four produces more than 3,000 gallons of greywater each month. See the potential?

If you're interested in saving, filtering and using your own greywater at home, there are a few details to keep in mind. First off, you don't want to use any toxic products which would contaminate that water.

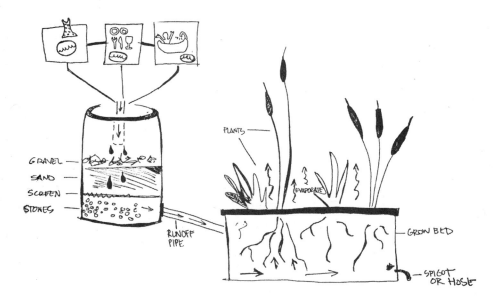

Basic Greywater Filtration System. CREDIT: NICOLE CALDWELL

That means no bleaches, artificial dyes, chemical perfumes or solvents. Of course, now that you've read *Better*, you're going to ditch all that stuff anyway, right?

Check the plumbing code where you live to see if it's possible to utilize recycled greywater for your flush toilets. Further precautions include adopting a control that will automatically flush the toilets if they sit too long (greywater can start to stink and become blackwater after just 24 hours of sitting) and filtering to keep things like hair out of the toilet system.

Below are instructions for creating a basic greywater filter that could easily be piped into the side of a raised garden bed or attached to a seepage hose for ongoing irrigation every time greywater is produced. If you attach your filter to a raised bed, be sure there is a hole at the opposite end of the bed to allow water to escape. Recommended plants for such an application are marsh plants (cattails, reeds or floating water plants like *Pistia stratiotes*), lilies, rosemary, sage and irises.

MATERIALS

- 55-gallon barrel (for smaller systems, you can use as small as a 5-gallon bucket)
- Plastic spigot
- Hose clamp
- Nylon hose
- Sand
- Crushed stone
- Weed mat, window screen or other mesh or filter
- Gravel
- Garden hose

INSTRUCTIONS

1. Install a spigot at the bottom of your barrel using a drill with appropriate-sized bit. Be sure to put a rubber washer between your spigot and the barrel to create a good seal.
2. Pour a 6-inch layer of stone into the barrel once your spigot is in place.
3. Put a sheet of weed mat (window screen or other mesh or filter) on top of the stone, cut to fit the circular barrel. Pour in a ten-inch layer of sand on top of the weed mat. Put a one-inch layer of gravel over top to hold the sand in place. This will be the filtering system of your greywater.
4. Divert your water. A discharge hose can go directly into the top of your drum with another hose attached to the bottom spigot. You can leave the spigot open with the hose running directly to plants or the ground, or it can go into another barrel for use later in the day. Be sure to use the water as soon as possible, as the bacteria present in the water will multiply quickly, which would make the water foul-smelling and unusable on edible plants.

Execute Small Space Gardening

You can still grow your own food if you don't have a lot of space. Square-foot and vertical gardens are tiny setups that offer big results. Best part? Setup can be done in less than an hour and for very little cash.

Square Foot Garden

A square foot garden is just what it sounds like. By planting in 1x1 square grids, you maximize growth potential. Each square unit can hold a head of cabbage, up to 16 carrots, onions or garlic heads, nine beets or one zucchini or tomato plant. Because you're using all of each square foot, you're not using as much space as you would in a traditional garden row.

MATERIALS

- Raised bed (Make your own with 2x10 lumber or scrap wood, bracing with 2x4s inside each corner to screw sides into. Be sure to use galvanized screws!)
- Grid (lattice, scrap wood or twine will work fine)
- Tape measure
- Screws
- Seeds or plants
- Soil

INSTRUCTIONS

1. Create a grid of 1x1 squares using a tape measure and twine, lattice or scrap wood. If you build your own lattice, simply use small screws at each crossing section.
2. Attach your grid to the raised bed with screws.
3. Utilize mulch gardening to fill your raised bed: a bottom layer of cardboard, then interchanging layers of compost, grass clippings, dead leaves, twigs and topsoil.
4. Space your plants or seeds. Each square foot can hold 16 small plants (3 inches between each), 9 medium plants (4 inches between each), 4 large plants (6 inches between each) or one extra-large plant.

Gutter Garden

A gutter garden will optimize space in any window in your house. If you have good light throughout larger rooms, gutter gardens can also function as space dividers or interesting sculptural pieces that can be hung from the ceiling. If you don't want to hang your gutters with wire or live in an area that has a lot of wind, you can mount them on an outside or inside wall with good sun exposure and a few gutter brackets. If you want to paint your gutters, do so after you've drilled drainage holes. Spray paint them first with a primer and follow with a heavy-duty, outdoor spray paint.

MATERIALS

- One section of eight-foot plastic rain gutter
- Six plastic gutter end caps
- Two steel cables cut to desired length for hanging gutters
- Six cross clamps to brace gutters and cable
- Six half-circle steel rods
- Two screw-in eye hooks (galvanized if gutter garden will be outside)
- Two crimping loop sleeves for cable
- PVC glue
- Drill with various bits
- Hacksaw
- Pliers
- Soil
- Seeds or plants
- Tape measure
- Permanent marker
- Level

INSTRUCTIONS

1. With your hacksaw, cut the length of gutter into three equal 32-inch pieces.
2. Glue gutter end caps to gutter lengths.
3. Flip the gutter pieces upside down and mark a straight line along the length of the center.
4. Using a drill bit the same size as the cable, make holes six inches in, on center from each gutter end for the cable to pass through.
5. Drill drainage holes with a large drill bit along the long center line on each gutter every few inches.

6. In your ceiling the same distance apart as cable rod holes in gutter, drill small pilot holes and screw in your eye hooks.
7. Make a loop with cable at top end and secure with crimping loop sleeves using pliers. Slide loops onto hooks. Slide cable through gutters from top to bottom. Use level to ensure gutters are hanging straight, and secure at desired heights with cross clamps and half-circle steel rods.
8. Add dirt to the gutters.
9. Plant seeds or add shallow-rooted plants to your gutters.
10. If your gutter garden is inside, be sure to lay a towel out under the bottom row when watering.

Note: This design is easy to modify for use in aquaponics, hydroponics or auto-watering systems.

Endnotes

INTRODUCTION

1. All references [online]. [cited February 18, 2015]. National World War II Museum fast facts. "What is a Victory Garden?" nationalww2museum. org/assets/pdfs/victory-garden-fact-sheet.pdf
2. 123HelpMe.com. "Children in the 1800s." 123HelpMe.com/view. asp?id=156574>; Nebraska Studies.org. "Pioneer Children: School." nebraskastudies.org/0500/frameset_reset.html?http://www.nebraska studies.org/0500/stories/0501_0207.html; US Department of the Interior Bureau of Land Management. "Kids on the Trail." blm.gov/or/oregontrail/ education-kids-trail.php; PBS, Ulysses S. Grant (film). "General Article: Kids in the Civil War." pbs.org/wgbh/americanexperience/features/general-article/ grant-kids/?flavour=mobile

CHAPTER 2

1. Glenn Albrecht "Environment Change, Distress & Human Emotion Solastalgia." TEDxSydney talk, 2010. [online]. [cited January 13, 2015]. youtube.com/watch?v=-GUGW8rOpLY
2. Chris Arsenault. "Top Soil Could Be Gone in 60 Years If Degradation Continues, UN Official Warns." Reuters, December 5, 2014. [online]. [cited February 2, 2015] huffingtonpost.com/2014/12/05/soil-degradation-un_ n_6276508.html
3. John Jeavons. *How to Grow More Vegetables (and Fruits, Nuts, Berries, Grains, and other Crops) Than You Ever Thought Possible on Less Land than You Can Imagine,* 8th ed. Ten Speed, 2012, p. 1.

4. New York City Department of Environmental Protection. Volume 2: Jamaica Bay Watershed Protection Plan. "Chapter Five Category 3, Stormwater Management Through Sound Land Use." October 1, 2007, p. 143. [online]. [cited February 2, 2015]. nyc.gov/html/dep/pdf/jamaica_bay/vol-2-chapter-5.pdf

5. Environment and Human Health, Inc. "Risks from Lawn Care Pesticides." [online]. [cited February 2, 2015]. ehhi.org/reports/lcpesticides/summary.shtml; US Fish & Wildlife Service. "Homeowners Guide to Protecting Frogs — Lawn and Garden Care." July 2000. [online]. [cited February 2, 2015]. fws.gov/Contaminants/DisplayLibrary.cfm?ID=5EA644DD-0437-276C-E59C3CA91C680887&Verify=0; US EPA. *Wild Ones Handbook,* "Today's Lawns." [online]. [cited February 2, 2015]. epa.gov/greenacres/wildones/handbk/wo8.html

6. All items [online]. [cited February 2, 2015]. Angie Wagner. "Las Vegas to Curb Water Use." Associated Press, April 1, 2003. community.seattletimes.nwsource.com/archive/?date=20030401&slug=vegas01; Ted Robbins. "Stakes High for Las Vegas Water Czar." NPR, June 13, 2007. npr.org/templates/story/story.php?storyId=10939792; Clark County Nevada. "Demographics." clarkcountynv.gov/depts/comprehensive_planning/demographics/Pages/default.aspx; Haya El Nasser. "Some big U.S. places find paradise in *not* being cities." *USA Today,* June 24, 2003. usatoday30.usatoday.com/news/nation/2003-06-24-cities-cover_x.htm.

7. Both items [online]. [cited February 2, 2015]. UN Framework Convention on Climate Change. *The Copenhagen Accord.* December 18, 2009. unfccc.int/resource/docs/2009/cop15/eng/l07.pdf; Bill McKibben. "Global Warming's Terrifying New Math." *Rolling Stone,* #1162 (July 19, 2012). rollingstone.com/politics/news/global-warmings-terrifying-new-math-20120719?page=2

CHAPTER 4

1. Global Footprint Network. "World Footprint." [online]. [cited February 3, 2015]. footprintnetwork.org/en/index.php/GFN/page/world_footprint/

2. Frances E. Kuo and William C. Sullivan. "Aggression and Violence in the Inner City: Effects of Environment via Mental Fatigue." *Environment and Behavior,* Vol. 33#4 (July 2001), pp. 543–571.

3. Bennu website. "greenpacks for great kids." [online]. [cited February 17, 2015]. bennuworld.com/gps-for-gks/; Bove's website. "Thank you!" [online]. [cited February 17, 2015]. boves.com/blog/2011/04/thank-you; Wendy Culverwell. "Bob's Red Mill founders give $1.35M." *Portland Business*

Journal January 31, 2011. [online]. [cited February 15, 2015]. bizjournals. com/portland/news/2011/01/31/bobs-red-mill-founders-fight-obesity. html; Maple Leaf Adventures. "Great Bear Rainforest Grizzly Bears Benefit from Adventure Tourism Donation." [online]. [cited February 17, 2015]. mapleleafadventures.com/about_maple_leaf/ecotourism-greatbearrain forest-1percent.php.

4. Sara Inés Calderón. "Activists Use Facebook to Help Pressure Nestlé on Deforestation Issue." *Ad Week,* March 23, 2010. [online]. [cited February 3, 2015]. adweek.com/socialtimes/activists-use-facebook-to-help-pressure-nestle-on-deforestation-issue/237474?red=if; Nestlé website. "Nestlé committed to traceable sustainable palm oil to ensure no-deforestation." October 30, 2012. [online]. [cited February 3, 2015]. nestle.com/media/ statements/update-on-deforestation-and-palm-oil.

5. SeaWorld Entertainment, Inc. "SeaWorld Entertainment, Inc. Reports First Quarter 2014 Results." May 14, 2014. [online], [cited February 3, 2015]. seaworldinvestors.com/news-releases/news-release-details/2014/ SeaWorld-Entertainment-Inc-Reports-First-Quarter-2014-Results/default. aspx

6. Octavio Blanco. "CEO Sea World is Stepping Down." CNN: Money, December 11, 2014 [online]. [cited February 3, 2015]. money.cnn. com/2014/12/11/news/companies/seaworld-atchison-ceo-resignation/

7. Barney Gimbel. "Attack of the wal-martyrs." *Fortune Magazine,* November 28, 2006, pp. 1–6. [online]. [cited February 3, 2015]. archive.fortune.com/ magazines/fortune/fortune_archive/2006/12/11/8395445/index.htm

8. See Erica L. Plambeck and Lyn Denend. "The Greening of Wal-Mart." *Stanford Social Innovation Review,* Spring 2008 citing "Twentieth Century Leadership," a speech by CEO Lee Scott on October 24, 2005. [online]. [cited February 3, 2015]. ssireview.org/articles/entry/the_greening_ of_wal_mart#comments

9. All references [online]. [cited February 17, 2015]. Newman's Own. "Charity." newmansown.com/charity/; Give Something Back Office Supplies. "A Kinder Corporation." givesomethingback.com/CustomLandingPage.aspx? cpi=Founders; Chipotle. "Food with Integrity?" chipotle.com/en-US/ fwi/fwi.aspx; Patriot Place. "Life is good." patriot-place.com/lifeisgood; Patagonia. "The Responsible Economy." patagonia.com/us/patagonia.go? assetid=1865

10. Richard Branson. "Richard Branson on Why Volunteer Work is Important for Business Leaders." *Entrepreneur,* October 8, 2012. [online]. [cited February 3, 2015]. entrepreneur.com/article/224549

11. Amie Schaenzer. "Naperville Business Owner Volunteers to Build New Parade Float for Local Non-Profit." Patch.com, June 5, 2014. [online]. [cited February 5, 2015]. patch.com/illinois/naperville/naperville-business-owner-volunteers-to-build-new-parade-float-for-local-nonprofit; Terri Gregory. "Naperville Small Business Leaders 'Do More' and Hold Fundraiser for WDSRA." Western DuPage Special Recreation Association, June 17, 2013. [online]. [cited February 3, 2015]. wdsra.com/Media/pdfs/Press-Releases/NapervilleTeamOneFundraiser.pdf

12. Joan Pryce. "Hospital Bosses Volunteer to Say Thank You." Heart of England NHS Trust. [online]. [cited February 3, 2015]. heartofengland.nhs.uk/hospital-bosses-volunteer/

13. Phyllis Smith. "Business Owners Teach High School Students About Giving Back." 5 News WDTV, January 16, 2015. [online]. [cited February 3, 2015]. wdtv.com/wdtv.cfm?func=view&section=5-News&item=Business-Owners-Teach-High-School-Students-About-Giving-Back-20643

CHAPTER 6

1. Both references [online]. [cited February 17, 2015]. Studio Roosegaarde. "Smart Highway." studioroosegaarde.net/project/smart-highway/info; Eve S. Mosher. "Seeding the City." evemosher.com/2011/seedingthe city/

2. Research into correlations between the arts and higher test scores, lower drug use, and improved health came from the following sources (all [online]. [cited February 4, 2015]): K. Vaughn and E. Winner. "SAT Scores of Students Who Study the Arts: What We Can and Cannot Conclude about the Association." *Journal of Aesthetic Education,* Vol. 34#3/4 (2000), pp. 77–89. artsedsearch.org/summaries/sat-scores-of-students-who-study-the-arts-what-we-can-and-cannot-conclude-about-the-association; Richard A. Friedman. "A Natural Fix for A.D.H.D." *The New York Times,* October 31, 2014. nytimes.com/2014/11/02/opinion/sunday/a-natural-fix-for-adhd.html?_r=0; H.L. Studkey and J. Nobel. "The Connection Between Art, Healing, and Public Health: A Review of Current Literature." *American Journal of Public Health,* Vol. 100#2 (February 2010), pp. 254–263. ncbi.nlm.nih.gov/pmc/articles/PMC2804629; Keith J. Petrie et al. "Effect of Written Emotional Expression on Immune Function in Patients with Human Immunodeficiency Virus Infection: A Randomized Trial." *Journal of Psychosomatic Medicine,* Volume 66#2 (March/April 2004), pp. 272–275. cdn.auckland.ac.nz/assets/fmhs/som/psychmed/petrie/docs/2004_HIV_writing_trial.pdf

3. US National Center for Education Statistics. *Arts Education in Public Elementary and Secondary Schools: 1999–2000 and 2009–2010.* US Department of Education, April 2012. nces.ed.gov/pubs2012/2012014rev. pdf; US Department of Education. "Prepared Remarks of U.S. Secretary of Education Arne Duncan on the Report, 'Arts Education in Public Elementary and Secondary Schools: 2009–10'." April 2, 2012. ed.gov/news/ speeches/prepared-remarks-us-secretary-education-arne-duncan-report-arts-education-public-eleme; Aggregate 2009 annual audited financial statements, CADAC (Canadian Arts Data/Données sur les arts au Canada), see p. 12 in *Creative Capital Gains: An Action Plan for Toronto:* toronto.ca/ static_files/economic_development_and_culture/docs/Sectors_Reports/ creative-capital-gains-report-august9.pdf; Sherri Welch. "Report says think about this: state spends $1 on arts and culture, which spends $51 on economy." *Crain's Detroit Business,* January 18, 2012. crainsdetroit.com/ article/20120118/FREE/120119879/report-says-think-about-this-state-spends-1-on-arts-and-culture; Americans for the Arts. *Art & Economic Prosperity III: The Economic Impact of Nonprofit Arts and Culture Organizations and Their Audiences,* page 1. americansforthearts.org/sites/ default/files/pdf/information_services/research/services/economic_ impact/aepiii/national_report.pdf. All above citations are [online]. [cited February 4, 2015].

CHAPTER 8

1. Jennifer Fink. Interview with the author, December 1, 2014.
2. Mayo Clinic website. "Nearly 7 in 10 Americans Take Prescription Drugs, Mayo Clinic, Olmsted Medical Center Find." Mayo Clinic News Releases, June 19, 2013. [online]. [cited February 5, 2015]. newsnetwork. mayoclinic.org/discussion/nearly-7-in-10-americans-take-prescription-drugs-mayo-clinic-olmsted-medical-center-find.
3. Kelly Rouba-Boyd. Interview with the author, November 25, 2014.
4. Jennifer Elizabeth Crone. Interview with the author. December 5, 2014.
5. Josey Baker. Interview with the author, December 3, 2014.
6. All references [online]. [cited February 18, 2015]. R. Kobau, et al. "Well-Being Assessment: An Evaluation of Well-Being Scales for Public Health and Population Estimates of Well-Being among US Adults." *Applied Psychology: Health and Well-Being,* Vol. 2#3 (November 2010), pp. 272–297. onlinelibrary.wiley.com/doi/10.1111/j.1758-0854.2010.01035.x/abstract; Emily Esfahani Smith. "There's More to Life Than Being Happy." *The Atlantic,* January 9, 2013. theatlantic.com/health/archive/2013/01/

theres-more-to-life-than-being-happy/266805/; Andrew Steptoe, Angus Deaton and Arthur A. Stone. "Subjective wellbeing, health, and ageing." *The Lancet,* November 5, 2014. thelancet.com/journals/lancet/article/PIIS0140-6736(13)61489-0/abstract; Barbara L. Fredrickson et al. "A functional genomic perspective on human well-being." Proceedings of the National Academy of Sciences. Vol. 110#33 (August 13, 2013), pp. 13684–13689. pnas.org/content/110/33/13684.full.pdf+html?sid=1077e571-6dae-41bc-a0a7-4a74590ac251

CHAPTER 9

1. Victor Frankl. *Man's Search for Meaning.* Beacon, 1959; Ed Diener and Martin E.P. Seligman. "Very Happy People." *Psychological Science,* Vol. 13#1 (January 2002). condor.depaul.edu/hstein/NAMGILES.pdf; Kennon M. Sheldon et al. "What is Satisfying About Satisfying Events? Testing 10 Candidate Pyschological Needs." *Journal of Personality and Social Psychology,* Vol. 80#2 (2001), pp. 325–339. apa.org/pubs/journals/releases/psp802325.pdf; Smith. "There's More to Life Than Being Happy."; Roy F. Baumeister et al. "Some Key Differences between a Happy Life and a Meaningful Life." *Journal of Positive Psychology,* Vol. 8#6 (2013), pp. 505–516. faculty-gsb.stanford.edu/aaker/pages/documents/SomeKeyDifferencesHappyLifeMeaningfulLife_2012.pdf. All citations [online]. [cited February 5, 2015].
2. Jan McColm. "A Hug a Day." *endeavors,* January 1, 2004. endeavors.unc.edu/win2004/hugs.html
3. Ferdinand Tönnies. *Gemeinschaft und Gesellschaft.* Nabu Press, 2010.
4. Sally Abrahms. "Introducing the Retirement Commune: When it comes to living arrangements, boomers are determined to get by with a little help from their friends." *The Boston Globe,* June 30, 2013. bostonglobe.com/magazine/2013/06/29/the-retirement-commune-housing-new-direction-for-baby-boomers/VO4KkbSUMv8JmcydfuuaHJ/story.html; Jim Fitzgerald for the Associated Press. "For the Aging, a Commune-like Alternative in NY." *Huffington Post,* February 28, 2013. huffingtonpost.com/2013/02/28/senior-assisted-living-commune-new-york_n_2781729.html; Jessica Salter. "Chickens Helping the Elderly Tackle Loneliness: A scheme to introduce hen keeping to the elderlyis turning out to have a miraculous effect on their wellbeing by reducing isolation and depression." *The Telegraph,* October 31, 2014. telegraph.co.uk/news/health/11198410/Chickens-helping-the-elderly-tackle-loneliness.html; Elise Hu. "Bay Area's Steep Housing Costs Spark Return to Communal

Living." NPR, December 19, 2013. npr.org/blogs/alltechconsidered/2013/12/19/250548681/bay-areas-steep-housing-costs-spark-return-to-communal-living; Nellie Bowles. "Tech Entrepreneurs Revive Communal Living." *San Francisco Gate,* November 18, 2013. sfgate.com/bayarea/article/Tech-entrepreneurs-revive-communal-living-4988388.php#page-1. All citations [online]. [cited February 5, 2015].

5. The Cohousing Association of the United States. *Cohousing Directory,* January 2015. [online]. [cited February 5, 2015]. cohousing.org/directory

6. Sir Albert Howard. *An Agricultural Testament.* Oxford, 1943, pp. 8–9. [online]. [cited February 5, 2015]. zetatalk3.com/docs/Agriculture/An_Agricultural_Testament_1943.pdf

7. Diane Cole. "Forget Facebook, Abandon Instagram, Move to a Village." Goats and Soda: Stories of Life in a Changing World, NPR, October 14, 2014.npr.org/blogs/goatsandsoda/2014/10/14/351254666/forget-facebook-abandon-instagram-move-to-a-village; Lisa Eadicicco. "Here's Why Office Layout Was So Important to Steve Jobs." *Business Insider,* October 7, 2014. businessinsider.com/steve-jobs-office-apple-pixar-2014–10. Both citations [online]. [cited February 6, 2015].

8. Kaiser Family Foundation. "Generation M2: Media in the Lives of 8- to 18-Year-Olds." National survey, 2010, p. 2. kff.org/other/event/generation-m2-media-in-the-lives-of; AVG Digital Diaries. "2014 Study." avg.com/digitaldiaries/homepage. Both citations [online]. [cited February 6, 2015].

9. Alexia D. Cooper et al. "Recidivism of Prisoners Released in 30 States in 2005: Patterns From 2005 to 2010." Bureau of Justice Statistics, April 22, 2014. bjs.gov/index.cfm?ty=pbdetail&iid=4986; Eliza Barclay. "Prison Gardens Help Inmates Grow Their Own Food—And Skills." The Salt, NPR, January 12, 2014. npr.org/blogs/thesalt/2014/01/12/261397333/prison-gardens-help-inmates-grow-their-own-food-and-skills; Bill Ritter. "Prison Gardens Grow New Lives for Inmates." ABC News, October 23, 2013. abcnews.go.com/blogs/lifestyle/2013/10/prison-gardens-grow-new-lives-for-inmates. All citations [online]. [cited February 6, 2015].

10.Julia Ernst. "Early Childhood Educators' Preferences and Perceptions Regarding Outdoor Settings as Learning Environments." North American Association for Environmental Education, Volume 2#1 (Winter 2014), p. 99. [online]. [cited February 6, 2015]. naaee.net/sites/default/files/publications/IJECEE/2nd/IJECEE%202(1)%20Winter%202014%20Issue.pdf

11.Dominique Mosbergen. "This 99-Year-Old Woman Makes a New Dress Every Single Day for a Child in Need." *The Huffington Post,* August 20,

2014. huffingtonpost.com/2014/08/20/99-year-old-dress-lillian-weber_
n_5694861.html; The Kindness Team website. Kindness Conversations.
thekindnessteam.org. Both citations [online]. [cited February 6, 2015].

CHAPTER 10

1. Ronda Kaysen. "Heard on the Street: E-I-E-I-O: New York City Backyards
Welcome Chickens and Bees." *The New York Times,* July 25, 2014. [on-
line]. [cited February 6, 2015]. nytimes.com/2014/07/27/realestate/
new-york-city-backyards-welcome-chickens-and-bees.html?_r=0

2. TerraChoice and Underwriters Laboratories. "The Sins of Greenwashing:
Home and Family Edition 2010," p. 6. [online]. [cited February 6, 2015].
sinsofgreenwashing.org/index35c6.pdf

3. Leonard Rice Engineers, Inc. et al. "Holistic Approach to Sustainable
Water Management in Northwest Douglas County," January 2007, p. 1.
[online]. [cited February 6, 2015]. cwcbweblink.state.co.us/WebLink/
ElectronicFile.aspx?docid=105705&&&dbid=0

4. John Hanc. "What the Doctor Ordered: Urban Farming." *The New York
Times,* November 6, 2014. nytimes.com/2014/11/07/giving/what-the-
doctor-ordered-urban-farming-.html; Manimugdha S. Sharma. "The Man
Who Made a Forest." *The Times of India,* April 1, 2012. timesofindia.india-
times.com/home/sunday-toi/special-report/The-man-who-made-a-forest/
articleshow/12488584.cms?referral=PM; Ben Christopher. "Aquaponics
Sprout a Business-Kijani Grows: Programmer reared in Kenya pairs aqua-
ponics, electronics in mission to feed the world." *San Francisco Chronicle,*
June 4, 2013. sfgate.com/homeandgarden/article/Aquaponics-sprout-a-
business-Kijani-Grows-4576219.php; Evofarm website. evofarm.com;
Fred de Sam Lazaro. "Re-Greening the Sahel." The Center for Investigative
Reporting, July 12, 2012. cironline.org/reports/re-greening-sahel-3643;
John Vidal. "Regreening Program to Restore One-Sixth of Ethiopia's Land."
The Guardian, October 30, 2014. theguardian.com/environment/2014/
oct/30/regreening-program-to-restore-land-across-one-sixth-of-ethiopia.
All Citations [online]. [cited February 6, 2015].

5. UN Conference on Trade and Development. *Wake Up Before It Is Too
Late: Make Agriculture Truly Sustainable Now For Food Security in a
Changing Climate.* Trade and Environment Review 2013. unctad.org/en/
pages/publicationwebflyer.aspx?publicationid=666; US Department of
Agriculture. "Family & Small Farms: A Time to Act." National Institute of
Food and Agriculture, January 27, 2010. csrees.usda.gov/nea/ag_systems/
in_focus/smallfarms_if_time.html; James MacDonald, Penni Korb and

Robert Hoppe. "Farm Size and the Organization of U.S. Crop Farming." Economic Research Report, United States Department of Agriculture, August 2013. ers.usda.gov/publications/err-economic-research-report/err152/report-summary.aspx. All Citations [online]. [cited February 6, 2015].

6. World Resources Institute. *Interactive Map of Eutrophication & Hypoxia.* [online]. [cited February 6, 2015] wri.org/our-work/project/eutrophication-and-hypoxia/interactive-map-eutrophication-hypoxia.

7. Patrik Grahn and Ulrika Stigsdotter. "The relation between perceived sensory dimensions of urban green space and stress restoration." *Landscape and Urban Planning,* Vol 94 (2010), p. 273. google.com/url?sa=t&rct=j&q=&esrc=s&source=web&cd=1&ved=0CB4QFjAA&url=http%3A%2F%2Fwww.researchgate.net%2Fpublication%2F222229937_The_relation_between_perceived_sensory_dimensions_of_urban_green_space_and_stress_restoration%2Flinks%2F09e4150ec1b46a823d000000.pdf&ei=L-THVJf6IdaQsQT6gYKYDQ&usg=AFQjCNF0hCETyF4xHS4DaZcS8D2la-3Izg&sig2=xvTjhMfR-TcC9j0h0fyhGg&bvm=bv.84349003,d.cWc; Christopher P. Niemic, Richard M. Ryan, and Edward L. Deci. "The Path Taken: Consequences of attaining intrinsic and extrinsic aspirations in post-college life." *Journal of Research and Personality,* Vol 73#3 (June 2009), pp. 291–306. ncbi.nlm.nih.gov/pmc/articles/PMC2736104/. Both citations [online]. [cited February 6, 2015].

8. Ruth Stout. *How to Have a Green Thumb Without an Aching Back: A New Method of Mulch Gardening.* Exposition Press, 1955.

CHAPTER 11

1. Henning Steinfeld at al. "Livestock's Long Shadow: Environmental issues and opinions." Food and Agriculture Organization of the United Nations, 2006, p. 4. fao.org/docrep/010/a0701e/a0701e00.htm; David Kaimowitz et al. "Hamburger Connection Fuels Amazon Destruction: Cattle ranching and deforestation in Brazil's Amazon." Center for International Forestry Research, 2004, p. 3. cifor.org/publications/pdf_files/media/Amazon.pdf. Both citations [online]. [cited February 9, 2015].

2. US Environmental Protection Agency. "Wastes-Resource Conservation-Common Wastes & Materials — Plastics." February 28, 2014. epa.gov/osw/conserve/materials/plastics.htm; World Centric website. "Frequently Asked Questions." wcback.worldcentric.org/about-us/faq; US Environmental Protection Agency. "Wastes-Resource Conservation-Common Wastes & Materials — Paper Recycling." June 10, 2014. epa.gov/wastes/conserve/

materials/paper; P.H. Gleick and H.S. Cooley. "Energy Implications of Bottled Water." *Environmental Research Letters* 4 (2009), February 19, 2009, p. 6. container-recycling.org/assets/pdfs/2009-BottledWaterEnergy. pdf. All citations [online]. [cited February 9, 2015].

3. Mark Bittman. "Is Junk Food Really Cheaper?" *The New York Times,* September 24, 2011. [online]. [cited February 9, 2015]. nytimes. com/2011/09/25/opinion/sunday/is-junk-food-really-cheaper.html? pagewanted=all

CHAPTER 12

1. Jackie Andrade. "What does doodling do?" *Applied Cognitive Psychology,* Vol. 24#1 (January 2010), pp. 100–106. [online]. [cited January 26, 2015]. pignottia.faculty.mjc.edu/math134/homework/doodlingCaseStudy. pdf

2. Robert A. Emmons and Michael E. McCullough. "Counting Blessings Versus Burdens: An Experimental Investigation of Gratitude and Subjective Well-Being in Daily Life." *Journal of Personality and Social Psychology,* 2003, Vol. 84#2 (2003), pp. 377–389. [online]. [cited February 20, 2015]. breakthroughealing.org/Documents/GratitudeStudy2003.pdf

Acknowledgments

THIS BOOK IS FOR DAD, Uncle Steve, Em and Emily, for slogging me through the Better Theory firsthand and teaching me the most terrible, important lessons of unconditional, timeless love.

Special thanks go to:

- My mother and sister, who made me understand that womanness is the same as humanness, and that true courage, beauty and grit lie in the deepest parts of every human heart
- The infallible extended Caldwell family, whose intellect, nerve and defiant sense of humor made me brave
- Bry, Rochelle, Rebekkah, Mrs. Hade, the Kenins and Goodmans, who served as the village that raised the girl
- My favorite cowgirls Aethena, Krumbein, Mollica, Stephy, Brittany, Julie, Carina, Beth, Jackie and Magoo — the toughest bunch of broads I'd follow into any foxhole, juke joint, gin mill or onto any cross-country bus ride
- Dev, Brett, Nils, Kip and Dilks for stopping at nothing to be all in with me through some of the most wonderful, terrifying and lovely experiences of my life
- Tony, Joe, Tambo, Nust, Andrew, Dan, Purwin, Hillman and Marco for making me who I would become
- Arnie, who showed me the kindness of strangers, the indestructible

relationship we can have with the Earth and who has tirelessly inspired me to trust my own conscience

- All you seekers who have visited and lived at Better Farm: You are the
  reason this work is possible
- Those North Country outlaws who turned a city girl into a coun-
  try girl and welcomed me with open arms: Carl, Scott, Fred, Bob,
  Walter, Reno, Doc, Sher, Holly, Erin, DJ, Aaron, Allen, AmberLee,
  Matt, Gerard, Glenn, Denise and Scotty
- New Society Publishers for believing in this work: Heather Nicholas,
  Ingrid Witvoet, EJ Hurst and the rest of that amazing staff
- My wonderful editor Betsy Nuse
- And to all you Han Solos, Sissy Hankshaws, Walkyres, Captain Kirks,
  Marianne Ravenwoods and Lady Amaltheas who every day don your
  superhumanness and set about making things better, more fun and
  more wild: I tip my cap to you.

Thank you.

Index

Page numbers in *italics* indicate photographs.

objectives of, 89
residents of, 69–73
sustainability education,
66–68, 140
Better Radio, 68, 98
Better Theory, 13–18, 104
betterArts
artists at, 93–96
community outreach, 96,
98–99
development of, 87–88
objectives of, 88
physical space for, 89–91
programs, 70
Bhutan, 52
biodiversity, 146
biomethane gas, 28
"Blackfish" (film), 50
Blue Field Writers House, 70–71
Bob's Red Mill Natural Foods, 48
body
exercise, 159–160
products used, 160
respect for, 153–154
Boname, Holly, *148, 178*
bottled water suppliers, 32
Bove's Cafe, 48
Bowser, Bob, 60–61, *61*, 62, 64
Brahmaputra River, 140
Branson, Richard, 51–52
British Medical Journal, 124
Brockman, Steve, 52
Brown, Mike, *78*
Brunch Club, 108
Buddhism, 109

businesses, sustainable practices,
45–53

C
Caldwell, Bill, 60, *60,* 62
Caldwell, Bob, *58,* 62
Caldwell, Dan, 38, 39, 58–59,
58
Caldwell, Kristen, 38–39, 66
Caldwell, Laura, 38
Caldwell, Steve, 39, 40, 41–42,
56–60, *58,* 62, 64–65, *66*
Caldwell family, 57, *58*
California, 31–32
Camelot Cohousing, 123–124
carbon dioxide, 33–34
Carr, Kevin, *92,* 93, *123, 143*
Chandra, Kiran, *86*
change, creating, 1–5, 9,
103–113
chicken coops, 193–196
chickens, 160–161
children
dependence on technology, 127
in nature, 129
China, methane use, 28
Chipotle, 51
Clement, AmberLee, *173*
climate change, 33–34
cohousing, 124
cold frames, 204–205
Collins, Jaci, *72, 81*
Colorado River, 32
Colorado Water Conservation,
138

About the Author

NICOLE CALDWELL is a self-taught envi-
ronmentalist, green-living savant and
sustainability educator with more than a decade of professional writing experience. She
is also the cofounder of Better Farm, a 65-
acre sustainability campus, organic farm and
artists' colony which serves as a blueprint for
environmentally conscious, creative living.
Better Farm attracts those who are interested
in doing *better* — growing from each experience, serving their communities and working
toward a gentler, healthier world. Better Farm
is home to the not-for-profit arts and music
outreach initiative betterArts; it works in
tandem with Better Farm to explore the intersection between sustain-
ability and art. Nicole's work has been featured in *Mother Earth News,
Reader's Digest, Time Out New York,* and many other publications. This
is her first book.

If you have enjoyed *Better,* you might also enjoy other

BOOKS TO BUILD A NEW SOCIETY

Our books provide positive solutions for people who want to
make a difference. We specialize in:

**Food & Gardening • Resilience • Sustainable Building
Climate Change • Energy • Health & Wellness • Sustainable Living**

**Environment & Economy • Progressive Leadership • Community
Educational & Parenting Resources**

New Society Publishers

ENVIRONMENTAL BENEFITS STATEMENT

New Society Publishers has chosen to produce this book on recycled paper made
with **100% post consumer waste,** processed chlorine free, and old growth free.
For every 5,000 books printed, New Society saves the following resources:[1]

25	Trees
2264	Pounds of Solid Waste
2491	Gallons of Water
3249	Kilowatt Hours of Electricity
4115	Pounds of Greenhouse Gases
18	Pounds of HAPs, VOCs, and AOX Combined
6	Cubic Yards of Landfill Space

[1]Environmental benefits are calculated based on research done by the Environmental Defense Fund
and other members of the Paper Task Force who study the environmental impacts of the paper
industry.

For a full list of NSP's titles, please call 1-800-567-6772 *or check out our website* at:

www.newsociety.com

new society
PUBLISHERS